RECLAIM YOUR
POWER

To Create Your Best Life

DANE STEVENS

An Extraordinary Life Publishing
33094 - 1583 Marine Dr.
West Vancouver, BC
Canada
V7V 4W7

www.anextraordinarylife.ca

ISBN
978-1-9991461-1-5 (Paperback)
978-1-9991461-0-8 (eBook)

Table of Contents

Disclaimer

There are no guarantees of healing from the use of the *Neuro Trauma Healing Process* or this book. If you or a loved one needs help, you may want to consider seeking help through a **physician, qualified mental health care provider, social worker**, or a **law enforcement agency**. You may also contact a **Crisis Hotline** or seek help at a **hospital emergency room** or **treatment center**. If you are currently in therapy, please consult with your mental health professional before you use any of the experiential exercises contained in this book. You may also get more information at:

www.reclaimyourpowerprocess.com or www.danestevensonline.com

Contact: info@danestevensonline.com

Dedication

I would like to dedicate this book to two father figures who have affected my life significantly, as well as the lives of many others. To my biological father, the late Albert Stevens, who showed me that inner transformation is possible. And to one of the founding fathers of the self-help movement, Dr. John Bradshaw, who was instrumental in my healing, this work, and in the unveiling of the science of healing the wounded Self. This book is dedicated to them and the many adults who still have wounded children running their lives.

FOREWORD

Humanity is experiencing a shift of epic proportions in its collective consciousness. More people than ever before are experiencing peaceful allowance; they live in harmony with life. The flame of awareness that is emitted from these individuals ignites a spark in all of us. It coaxes, encourages, and gives us permission to follow our own desire to move back a little closer to our own truest nature. And when that flame within us is reignited, it radiates out into our families and communities, and in turn benefits all humanity. Could this simple, easy, natural freedom be called enlightenment? If it is, then enlightenment is no longer an experience achieved exclusively by saints, monks, gurus and the like. It is available to us all—it is a birthright.

Remarkably, at the very same time of this momentous awakening, we are also seeing more people than ever before who are debilitated by the effects of trauma. In our ecosystem of interconnectedness, there are no coincidences—these concurrent events go hand in hand. Spiritual leaders have asked the question: do we need to suffer in order to find the momentum and the motivation to grow spiritually, to awaken—to be happy?

I believe we are all being called back to our divine Self regardless of whether we are living an angst-ridden life or a pleasant one. But it is those who are suffering who hear the call to peace most loudly and clearly, for it is they who have been further separated from who they truly are. Without suffering, it would be necessary to listen very closely for the call, as it could be easily overlooked and the tremendous opportunity to awaken missed. It is through suffering that our hearts open and seek truth, healing and change.

Dane once said to me: "Enlightenment? I think it's really just letting go of the heaviness."

Anyone suffering the effects of past trauma knows first-hand how heavy a burden it is. It is a weight that is constantly being carried into every aspect of life. It is a burden that must be let go of in order to rise. In *Reclaim Your Power*, Dane Stevens offers a revolutionary process of healing that not only safely heals trauma but also links healing to the spiritual path of growth. He shows us how to set the burden down and open our hearts to transformation.

You picked this book up for a reason—you allowed it to find you. This is your call, clear and in black and white. Hearing the call means the healing has already begun and the hardest part is over.

Freedom starts from right here, right where you are sitting in this present moment. In opening this book, you have opened a gate that has the potential to lead you on one of the greatest journeys of your life. You need only take that first courageous step of reading on. The *Neuro Trauma Healing Process* contains within it a Soul's journey, a journey of remembrance and reuniting—reclaiming. It is a journey of returning to your truest nature of inner peace and happiness. If you choose to start down this path, you will reach inside, into the corners and crevices of your innermost being, bring your past out into the sunshine and make peace with it. It will take courage, but it will be worth it.

If inner peace were the only thing you were to find through taking this journey, it would be enough, but your healing has a power to evoke trans-formation in the world. Like the symbiotic relationship of bee to flower, your healing pollinates the healing of others and produces the honey-sweetness of positive change for all humanity.

~Anne Babchuk – Senior Facilitator NTHP

RECLAIM YOUR POWER

To Create Your Best Life

INTRODUCTION

Welcome to *Reclaim Your Power*. This book is an introduction to the **Neuro Trauma Healing Process (NTHP)**, a process that has the ability to deal with and heal simple negative patterns and unwanted behaviors, as well as deep, major, past traumas. This book is also an account of a long journey of healing that led me to the creation of this work.

The *Neuro Trauma Healing Process* was developed purely out of necessity. I went through and overcame an early childhood trauma that plagued me for the majority of my adult life. It was a series of modalities, research, and personal and spiritual growth experiences that led me to the development of this safe, gentle and profoundly effective healing process. This book is the culmination of the unique set of experiences that took place on my path to becoming free—free from my past. It will show you how you, too, can free your Self. This work has been a great gift to me and I feel it is my duty, as well as my honor, to pass it on to others.

The title *Reclaim Your Power* ultimately says it all. We are born with innate power, the power of creativity and choice. It aligns us with the wisdom and majesty of the universe. Unfortunately, many people have involuntarily and unknowingly pushed their power to the deepest recesses of their psyche. Life experiences have caused them to bury it, to hide or ignore it and—worst of all—to forget it. Far too many of us have forgotten who we truly are.

You can now reclaim the power that has been lost to your past. You start this by slowing down the chatter from the negative tapes that have been continually running, involuntarily, within you. By slowing down and even stopping these tapes, you will create space within you. Space equals peace, and peace equals harmony. Harmony is being in alignment and agreement with who you really are—who you deep inside, know yourself to be. The power may feel unavailable, inaccessible or perhaps even non-existent to you right now, but I can assure you it is there waiting to be uncovered, remembered and revived. That is what this book and the process contained within it will show you how to do—reclaim the power that is rightly and inherently yours. You will have the ability to bring your past issues to a full and complete resolution—for good.

You will have the ability to bring your past issues to a full and complete resolution—for good.

THE NEXT STEP IN OUR HEALING AND DEVELOPMENT

I consider the *Neuro Trauma Healing Process* the next step in the evolution of our psychological healing and spiritual development. I say that because of what it shows us about how we *work* as human beings; how intertwined our physiological, psychological and spiritual selves are, and the science of how these three aspects of our being all work together—or don't. *NTHP* experientially reveals to us how interconnected our mental and emotional state is to how we experience the world. It shows us that the very cause of ongoing negative mental and emotional occurrences in our life come from past adverse experiences trapped in our body. *NTHP* gives us the ability to safely align with the energy of the past event inside us and create a relationship with our younger Self—at the time it happened. Through developing and nurturing this inner relationship, we will be naturally led from the fear and adversity of that time, back to our nature in present time—growing and thriving in our life. We learn that the inner relationship itself is the key to our healing and proves to us that life truly is an inside job.

When I say this is the next step in the evolution of our healing it is not meant to imply that other healing modalities are ineffective or wrong, quite the contrary. It is simply showing us that this is another step forward from all we have learned; a step that has, until now, been missing. This step not only shows us that we can fully heal from our past, but that our pain and suffering has had purpose and is actually a portal to the higher consciousness within us.

Talk therapy helps us to understand our stories and make sense of what happened to us. It is very valuable to communicate; to be heard and understood by someone who echoes our experiences back to us in empathy, and who possibly shows us a new perspective. The *EMDR* (Eye Movement Desensitization and Reprocessing) modality then shows us that visuals of highly emotional events of our past are held in the body as sensation and can be brought back into consciousness through left/right brain processing. Modalities like *NLP* (Neuro-Linguistic Programming) and *EFT* (Emotional Freedom Technique) go on to reveal to us how these negative past events held in our nervous system can be felt and positively affected by way of outer physical application. *Hypnotherapy* gives us the ability to go back in time and connect with the part of ourselves that still feels stuck, hurt, wounded or scared. And *SE* (Somatic Experiencing) shows us that support, nurturing and compassion raises the level of trust with the inner life that makes sustainable healing possible.

The *Neuro Trauma Healing Process* involves aspects of all of these modalities, wrapped simply within one guiding principal: Relationship—a relationship that has not been directly accessible to us. This is the next step I am referring to: creating a trusted, intimate rapport with the life within us. *NTHP* shows us that through the building of this relationship we can connect with the root cause or false belief that is creating our dysfunctional experience(s). Connecting with where this cause or belief came from gives us the ability to experience it anew and re-choose our response to it. By understanding *what* it is and *why* it is there, we can offer the necessary love, support and assistance to bring that inner part of us back into the safety of the present moment, where *it is not happening anymore.*

When the inner realization occurs that the past experience is not happening anymore, it ceases to operate within us at a subconscious level, and the outer negative pattern stops happening. This shows us that the relationship itself is the healing. Like any relationship, if nurtured consistently, it will continue to evolve, grow deeper and become more harmonious and loving over time.

This process proves to us how we work. That what is going on inside of us at the subconscious level is responsible for our outer experience of the world. When this is realized and *NTHP* is utilized fully, it will heal us from our past and resolve trauma. It allows us to consciously process the negative experiences and restrictive beliefs that have been stuck, looping in our nervous system. We do not have to be at the mercy of the subconscious mind and bullied into dysfunction any longer. These unconscious parts of ourselves have been available to us the whole time, we just have not known how to access them. *NTHP* will lead us into Self-empowerment, or choice, with certainty. The only thing that will stop the process from working is if we choose to stop it ourselves.

ENDING DESTRUCTIVE CYCLES

– The *NTHP* gives us direct access to the subconscious mind and the ability to heal our past in a simple, safe and efficient manner. This healing automatically opens up the avenue that connects us to what I will refer to as our *Authentic Self*, or our *higher consciousness*.

NTHP levels the playing field by showing us we are all similar in our makeup. What we have been taught to believe about *success or failure* and *better or worse* comes from societal programming. Programming that is born out of ignorance—without the understanding of how we work. The fact is, we are all dealing with a mind and a nervous system of which very little has been known about or taught. You could say the nervous system is the determining factor of our fate.

We are seeing the domino effect of trauma running rampant in all levels of society today. No one is exempt from the far-reaching ripple effect of trauma. The majority of us will experience some form of trauma in our life. It has been said: *It's not a matter of if you will experience a trauma, but a matter of when.* Many of us have been subjected to varying degrees of neglect, abuse and violence in life. These experiences—left unaddressed, can leave a person with feelings of low self-worth, fear, anger or mental and emotional pain. It doesn't matter where we come from (social status, cultural heritage or family dynamic), unless we have an understanding of this aspect of what makes us up, living with an unresolved trauma can make our life seem like a throw of the dice—risky and with an uncertain outcome. Left unaddressed, these emotions and behaviors will continue to fester and out-picture themselves, automatically being passed on to our children, loved ones and into our communities. Add to the mix accidents, natural disasters and the devastating effect of war, and we have a self-perpetuating tornado of trauma. This work shows why we are experiencing what we are experiencing in our life and has the ability to put an end to passing these destructive cycles on.

There are an insurmountable number of people who are walking around wounded in the world. These are people who have trauma(s) actively looping in their nervous systems. These traumas are coming out in their life as negative patterns, chronic conditions, unwanted behaviors, addiction, instability, anxiety and fear. Most do not know how to deal with or release them. Many people dealing with these dysfunctions in their lives have no idea why they are even happening to them, or how they are running and ruining their lives. They just know that they are in pain and want to get out of it.

Trauma is now getting the attention that it needs, but how to actually heal it (bring it to resolution and stop the pattern) has not been understood. With the awareness this process brings us, we see that we no longer have to live with a past that negatively affects our life. This work is the ultimate voyage in Self-discovery. It is science-based in that it uses left- and right-brain processing to *unfreeze* information that has been stuck looping in the nervous system. But this work is experiential. Like the science of quantum physics, when doing this process we become a part of the equation. This means that the only one who can prove its effectiveness to us is *us!* We are the subject from whom the material comes, and are the *experiencer* of the evidence. This book is not about learning more—we already know way too much. It's about un-learning and getting back to what is real and true for us. Nor is it about being told what to do. Through this work, you will discover that you have all of your answers within you. *NTHP* will prove to you that what is going on within you at the level of the nervous system is what creates your outer experience in the world. It will show you that you are, in fact, creating your life. With *NTHP,* you will be given the ability to heal from these past circumstances that have lodged themselves in your unconscious and are negatively impacting your life.

WHO IS THIS BOOK FOR?

Initially, I set out to write this book specifically for those who have negative experiences from their past that have turned into a life sentence. I wanted to tell them there is a way out. But the process turned out to be much more creative and empowering than I first realized, and it is actually for anyone wanting fundamental change and to experience a higher degree of conscious awareness and freedom of choice in their life. I want to bring *NTHP* to anyone who is limited by the experiences of their past so they, too, can move beyond it, into the power of the present moment.

Everyone could benefit from this work, but it is important to note that not everyone is open or ready for it. One must be at a place in their journey of healing to be able to accept and follow the guidance that comes from within the work. If you are open, willing and ready for change, this book is for you and will put you on the path of healing.

- If you have been living with a chronic condition, addiction or any sort of dis–ease that you have not been able to resolve, this book is for you.

- If you are stuck, frustrated and feel unable to break free of a negative pattern somewhere in your life, whether it is with health, finances, relationships, career or self-worth, you will benefit from this book.

- If you are a therapist, counselor or healer, this book is for you. You should be informed of and ultimately trained in this process. Not only will your client's benefit from the phenomenal results it generates, but you will too. As a matter of fact, the facilitator's healing must come first.

- If you are seeking true and lasting freedom in your life, this guide-book will give you the foundation required to put you clearly on your personal path.

NTHP has brought relief to many lives. Here are some examples of what people have used NTHP to deal with and heal:

- Chronic pain

- Addiction

- Depression and anxiety

- Obesity / eating disorders

- Fear

- Insomnia

- PTSD

- Chronic health issues

- Self-sabotage

- Low self-worth/ self-esteem

- Cluttering and hoarding

- Heart conditions and dis-ease

- Relationship issues

- Financial issues

- Creative blocks

The vast majority of people in the world today have a degree of what is termed *trauma*. What that means is they have something unprocessed and stuck, looping in their nervous system creating a negative pattern or dysfunction in their life. We all want to be free of negative patterns, become whole and live healthy, successful, fully expressed lives. However, the truth of the matter is we cannot skip steps. We cannot skip addressing the core reason or the cause for our condition before it can be resolved. Only then will we be able to move into living our true potential. I completely understand the desire to "just move on." I have had many clients try to jump ahead, only for them to come to the awareness that without a solid and true foundation nothing will stay standing. This process will develop that foundation.

"It's not a matter of if you will experience trauma, but a matter of when."

I am very passionate about this work because of what it did for me, and for the great success I have had facilitating the process with other people. If I am making the process sound like a magic pill or a cure-all (and I have to admit that sometimes it feels like it is), I want to be clear and up-front on a couple of things so no one feels misled. The first is that this is not a quick fix. Yes, the process will put you on the fast track to healing, but it is based on inner compassionate connection and—like the building of any healthy relationship—it takes time and effort.

The second is that this is a *person–centered approach*, meaning that, even though you will need the help of a facilitator at the start, the answers come from inside *you*. You have all the answers to all the questions about your healing and empowerment, you just have not known how to access them. You will find that your healing comes primarily from the inner connection itself. This connection then opens up into higher consciousness within you.

I also want to be clear on the fact that this process is not a theory, a coping skill, a technique to overcome or a way to compensate. It is a process that will give you direct access to your subconscious mind. The subconscious is by far your most powerful creative faculty, and it is what holds the keys to your personal wellness. Connecting to this inner place with consistency and compassion will bring you to a full and complete healing of negative patterns. And here we go with the magic again: there is nothing for you to do except allow the process to work through you. Healing happens within the process and within the work, the foundation of which is the connection to, and relationship with, your inner life. Your outer-world experience will wrap around your inner-world experience. It has to, because it is just mirroring what is going on inside of you. While this all sounds very mystical, if not ethereal, you will see that it is very simple, practical and functional work, and you stay in a place of safety and control while doing it.

THE TWO PREREQUISITES

1. **Be open-minded.**

   This is abstract work, it is not lineal. If you happen to be left-brain dominant—a person driven by logic and control—you will have to suspend your judgments and any tendency you have to over-analyze. In order to make way for the process to work, you don't have to believe something that you do not, you simply suspend any judgment that may arise. Just follow the process and let it show you. If you can put yourself in a place of trust or receptivity for even a short time, the process will show you, without any doubt, that it is working.

2. **Be open to the possibility that you are responsible for your life.**

   As you do this process, you will be shown how you are creating your life. This is not about blame but is the starting point of reclaiming your power. To tell someone they are responsible for the pain they are experiencing may seem like a ridiculous, even cruel, thing to say. Especially to someone who is, or has been, at the receiving end of severe abuse, even more so if they were a child or infant at the time it happened. So, please understand what I am saying here: *it is the memory of a past negative experience that is still alive within you that is creating the pain and the dysfunctional pattern or behavior in your life.* You can now change your response to the memory that has been operating inside you, and therefore change your current experience. It is imperative that you realize that, to the life inside of you, the negative event is still happening. When you have an understanding of this reality and show compassion for yourself, you are taking responsibility for your life and are at the starting point to begin your work.

   Congratulations, it took a very strong Soul to go through what you have gone through, and you are here now. Welcome to the beginning of your journey to freedom.

Client Testimonial:

I was surprised at the revelations that were brought to the forefront of my mind. I feel that I have been able to address the key events behind some of the things holding me back because of life experiences in my youth. [NTHP] has helped me both to forgive and find forgiveness. I feel great relief from the stresses in my life as well as from physical pain.

MY STORY

I grew up in a beautiful little town in the interior of British Columbia, Canada. I am the middle child of three. My parents raised my brother, my sister and me with a lot of encouragement and involvement in sports, both in and out of school. Growing up, my father had not been allowed to play sports himself, so he did the obvious thing to make up for it. He opened his own sports shop. This kept my parents extremely busy, and us kids involved in a myriad of different activities and fully equipped with whatever sports gear we needed.

We definitely had our challenges and faults as a family, but there is no question in my mind that my parents loved us and had our best interests at heart when it came to our upbringing. They worked very hard to provide a comfortable home with all the amenities we needed, and all the recreation we could have dreamed of. This did, however, mean my siblings and I had a lot of unsupervised time while my parents worked. Being the '70s, this was not unusual and our neighborhood was considered a very safe place, so much so that our back door was never locked.

Then, at six years of age, that security for me was breached and silently shattered. I experienced a series of events that created a deep sense of shame within me that would have an enormous impact on the next thirty-five years of my life. Over a two-year period, an older boy in my neighborhood repeatedly took advantage of me sexually. He was the big kid on the block who I looked up to, admired and always wanted to hang around. This made what he did very confusing and conflictingly painful for me. So confusing that I kept it a secret from everyone. The confusion and shame I felt was too complex for me to handle, and because of this I *forgot*—that is, I managed to block the experience out of my memory—for over sixteen years.

With that memory buried deeply within me, the next chapters of my life went on seemingly normally, but as I look back I see many indicators of compensation for the shame that lay unattended within me. I cried out for help by getting in trouble at school. I stopped myself from achieving success in my academic life as well as in my sports life, which I loved, and I self-medicated with marijuana. The shame lay hidden at the base of all the decisions I made and kept me from being able to move forward by continually sabotaging my own success.

In my early twenties, I had my first real love relationship. It was a beautiful, tumultuous, sweet, heart-wrenching, exciting and confusing mixture of emotions, as most young loves usually are. We were together for a year and a half and became engaged in that time. Many insecurities were brought up in both of us, and when we eventually broke up my heart was shattered. I did not handle it well. I was in very rough shape and felt as if my soul was bleeding. In short, I was a complete mess. The tears were flowing, my heart was hurting and I was trying to make sense of what was going on with me. It made me wonder just what kind of weak and ridiculous romantic I was. The truth is, what came out at that time was all of the pent-up and blocked-out energy I had forced down from the events that happened to me between the ages of six and eight. My emotions ran rampant like never before, and the energy of those childhood events came back to me with a vengeance. I remembered what happened. The memories that came up shook me; I did not know what to do with them. Whether I wanted to admit it or not, that period between the ages of six and eight was actually when I had my first intimate relationship. These similar feelings of intimacy with my fiancé triggered the past that carried such deep pain and brought them all to the surface. As difficult as this experience was, it would turn out to be a great catalyst of growth for me.

The next years of my life were dedicated to dealing with the energy that had been awakened in me. Through the guidance of a counselor, I was introduced to the valuable idea of meditation. I started spending hours meditating and *being* in nature. It was helpful, but I was not guided to do my inner work, and did not have the understanding of the importance of doing so. Thus, what was going on inside of me was not properly addressed.

By the age of thirty-six I had some life experience, learned about spiritual principals and had started to look inward for answers. I had a strong practice in meditation and, through metaphysical study, learned about my ability to create and manifest the things I wanted in my life. I appeared to be doing very well. I had a successful business with great employees. I was making good money and doing some traveling. I was living in a beautiful place just off the ocean and driving my vehicle of choice. The outer appearance all looked very good.

The one thing that indicated something was wrong was that my intimate love relationships were very short-lived. I would end relationships prematurely and then immediately seek out intimacy elsewhere. The connection I was craving always seemed to elude me. It made me ask, *why?* Why, when I was feeling so strong and successful in all other areas of my life was I consistently preventing myself from having a satisfying long-term intimate relationship? Was I not meeting the right women? Was it not my time, or... was there something wrong with me? Having asked the question, I knew that I had to check into it. It forced me to look at the sexual abuse I experienced as a child.

I went to a few support groups and, for a period of time, received some counseling. Neither seemed to work for me. A gentleman who was an acquaintance from one of the support groups recommended a therapist to me who was also a healer. I was eager and open to try anything that might set me on the right track, so I followed up on his recommendation.

When I met this healer, I had little knowledge of trauma, energy or healing, and went into our sessions trusting in her expertise. A few sessions in, she said I had an *energy cirque* around my sexual region, which sounded reasonable considering what I was dealing with. She asked if I would like to "take it out?" Explaining to me that it was like "going for a homerun." Who doesn't want to hit a homerun?! I agreed, and she proceeded to try and force the hidden trauma out of me. What she failed to mention, or didn't know, was that in trying to force the trauma out there is a possibility of hitting a foul ball. It did not go well.

In short, the healer was not equipped to handle the trauma that was to come out from inside me. She had been performing some cranial sacral work on me, as well as hands-on bodywork where she had me up on a table and contorted in different positions. I recall that at one point she had me pinned down in a pretzeled-up, twisted position, was leaning over on top of me and urging me to: "Go there, go there!" This is when the energy cirque she spoke of broke, and I became instantly frightened for no apparent reason. I remember it clearly to this day. I first lost complete awareness of where I was, and which way was up or down. When I came back, I felt as if

I had been plugged into a 220-volt electrical outlet. Frenetic energy surged through me making me feel like I had jittery platelets. I thought the energy would dissipate and eventually fade away, but it did not. It only got worse.

Over a very short period of time I went from standing on solid ground in my life to being completely unstable. My nervous system had been unhinged and was running wild; I felt completely out of control. I was deeply fearful throughout the days after this episode, and over time my world began to mirror this.

My life literally began to fall apart and crumble around me. Everything that was good and strong, everything I had built, began to slip away. I started losing clients and contracts left and right and the sale of a business fell through. Worst of all, I lost my solid inner connection to Self. I was watching my life quickly turn into a complete and utter shambles.

After many months of work with the healer I ran out of money, and she refused to see me any longer. While this enraged me, it was clear that she was panicked and did not know what she had done or how to fix what had happened. I remember demanding: "You can't leave me like this!" But the damage was already done.

I am not going to go into the details of what happened in my life after that, but I will say that I went from living a very comfortable, what would be considered successful life, to being broke within two years and homeless within three.

This sent me on a frantic search to figure out what had happened, what was continuing to happen to me, and how to get my life back. I saw a number of therapists, counselors and healers over the next four years, but none of them had any understanding of what had happened to me, or what to do.

I tried *Talk Therapy, Gestalt, Hypnotherapy, EMDR*, and a number of other modalities. I found them all to be great tools that gave me insight into, and understanding of, my story, but none gave me any lasting relief. My nervous system continued to run out of control on a rampage that kept me from having any stability in my life.

After five years of searching I finally found someone who had some understanding of trauma and how to safely approach it. Hazel Williams-Carter, a trauma specialist, understood what happened to me; ironically, because she had the same experience with a healer as I did. Hearing of her experience alone gave me the first glimpse of hope and my first advancement towards relief.

Through Peter Levine's *Somatic Experiencing* approach, Hazel taught me about the workings of the nervous system and the effects of trauma on it. Meeting her was the impetus for undoing the damage done by the initial healer, as well as the start of my journey into understanding what trauma is and how it works.

While I experienced some much needed understanding and relief in working with Hazel, it wasn't until I became familiar with Dr. John Bradshaw's teachings that an intimate connection to the actual source of my fear was made. Dr. Bradshaw's process of connecting with the inner child through alternate handwriting gave me direct access to the part of me that continued to be scared and reactive.

To my amazement, I found that through this practice I was able to make direct contact with the "sub," or unconscious, part of me that was the source and cause of the enormous fear that had taken over my life. I worked diligently on my own at connecting to and healing this part of me. Unfortunately, I ended up very frustrated at trying to convince the child within me that he was now safe. My joyful anticipation turned into an eight-month battle with myself! I knew that the presence of this wounded part of me was there and real, and that I could communicate with him. For some reason, though, I was unable to create a safe or stable enough relationship with him to move out of fear and instability to heal.

Up to this point I had been working on my own, and I could not find my way through it. I was frustrated, exhausted and angry. So, what then? I still wasn't out of the woods. I searched high and low for anyone who did this type of work. I found no one. I even attempted to convince a few counselors to try it with me, to no avail. I scoured the internet and called many prospective therapists. Still, I couldn't find anyone willing to work with me in this way. Then, six years after originally having my nervous system unhinged and my life flooded with fear, I found someone that would help me with the work I had been exploring. Her name was Mary Hoffman, who was fatefully living just down the road from where I was staying at the time.

Mary had done alternate handwriting work before. It was the same approach I had been using over the past months, but it was not until I worked with another person that I was able to access the areas of my subconscious that needed to be reached. She had the outside perspective that was needed to ask the questions I was blind to or was unable to ask.

It only took two months of working with Mary for me to *untangle* myself and gain *traction*. I was then able to successfully take the practice on myself and continue to build the relationship within me and allow it to flourish. I was on the fast track to feeling safe and at peace.

The Albert Einstein quote about not being able to change something from the same level of thought that created it took on a whole new level of meaning for me.

> *No problem can be solved by the*
> *same kind of thinking that created it.*
>
> *~ Albert Einstein*

I continued on, committed to connecting with my inner life on a daily basis through writing and a committed meditation practice. What came out of this was more than I could ever have imagined. I was able to completely *unfreeze* the traumas from my past and was taken to the point of having a completely healthy relationship with my Inner Self. This newfound relationship was based in trust, and it allowed me the freedom of complete Self-expression. I was finally able to accept myself completely. With all the different aspects of healing that I learned and had incorporated into my daily discipline, what naturally evolved was a gentle, safe and highly effective method of treating trauma.

I had not intended to develop this process, it seemed to just develop itself. It is so natural and effective that I cannot help but liken it to electricity. It has always been here, we just needed to *discover* it to actively utilize it.

I have called this method the **Neuro Trauma Healing Process (NTHP)**. By no means do I take sole credit for the foundation of this work. Truth be told, the part of the process in which we access the subconscious mind through the left/right-brain technique has been known about for decades. But this is the first time it has been developed into a comprehensive functional process. NTHP incorporates a trained facilitator who gently directs their client through the maze of the subconscious by using left/right-brain exercises and guided meditations with a *person-centered approach* to ensure a safe and powerful experience.

I am grateful for, and forever indebted to, Hazel Williams-Carter, Dr. Peter Levine, Mary Hoffman and Dr. John Bradshaw, for without their wisdom, guidance and love, I would not be where I am today, presenting this material to you now. I now live free of shame and free of the erroneous beliefs I had previously built around myself. Life now flows through me naturally, happily and abundantly.

Now, I am happy to introduce the most direct, the safest, and—by far, the most effective modality I know of for the treatment of trauma: The *Neuro Trauma Healing Process*. I believe it is the most powerful tool that we have for this type of work. I feel I can safely say this because of what I have personally experienced, and because of what I have seen with clients.

It is the only modality I know of that:

- Gives safe and direct contact with the unconscious mind.

- Creates a tangible, ongoing relationship with your inner life.

- Allows *you* to get your answers from within *you*.

- Gives a sense of control; therefore, true Self-empowerment.

- Creates sustainable healing.

> *I don't know how to heal you or what you need—*
> *but I do know that you do.*

THE GOAL

It is time for this process to become a recognized and utilized method in the field of psychological and spiritual healing. What I experienced in the form of trauma has millions of people gripped in its clutches right now. My mission? To inform people that recovery is now attainable. Your past and the resulting dysfunction(s) do not have to be permanently debilitating. This is a highly effective way of not only healing and bringing inner peace and harmony to your life, but also of becoming wonderfully powerful and creatively free as well.

My goal is to have the *NTHP* teaching mandatory learning for anyone in a healing field: psychologists, therapists, counselors, teachers, healers and body workers so that:

- Those working closely with others do not unknowingly traumatize them further.

- Those working closely with others can spot, and know how to help, a person who has just been traumatized, or has been triggered from an old trauma.

- We can stop the cycles of abuse and make our world a better, more fulfilling and safer place to be.

By helping to heal the great number of emotionally wounded people there are in the world, we can help our society to evolve. We can grow up safely. And we can live the free, happy and fully expressed lives we came here to live. For me, this is simply paying it forward.

We have the answers for everything
we need and desire within us.

With love and compassion,

Dane Stevens

Part 1

UNDERSTANDING TRAUMA & THE PROCESS OF HEALING

FIGHTING SHADOWS IN THE DARK

The original title of this book was going to be *Fighting Shadows in the Dark*, because that is what dealing with a trauma can feel like. It is so hard to uncover and deal with an issue that we cannot see clearly or get a hold of. It is like grasping for something in the dark that we do not want to touch, but know we have to in order to regain control of our life.

Trauma can also be described like trying to drive a car while looking in the rear-view mirror. It is very difficult, if not impossible, to stay on the road and move forward if we are continually forced to look backward. This is what trauma does to us: it forces us to look back. It steals the present moment from us and takes us away from what is really happening. In extreme cases it pushes us off the road and causes us to crash. It threatens to destroy what we have managed to build in our life to that point. It is a very stressful way to live.

A key factor to successful living is being fully present in the moment, and that comes first and foremost by being at peace. This means feeling safe and secure, and fully accepting of our Self. If we do not feel safe, secure and at peace with our Self, then we must do the inner work required to heal and transform what has been going on inside. If we do not, then we will be constantly pulled out of any peace and alignment we build for our Self. If the peace and security we are seeking comes from outside us, it is temporary and will be fleeting.

The goal in *NTHP* is to resolve the past, not to forget, get rid of, overcome or deny it. Understandably, most people with negative conditions want to be rid of them. Yes, the dysfunctions we feel and experience are a direct result of that past, but the past is still going on inside us today! It will not be put to rest simply by telling it to or by heartily ignoring it.

The question to ask our Self is not: "How do I get rid of this?" but: "What is this?" This is the question that will point us in the direction of true and lasting healing. Realize that to try and get rid of *it* is to deny *it*; this denial creates more separation and conflict within us. This *it* is a part of us! It is the part of us that has been hurt, confused, wounded or wronged, that has become an entity unto itself within us. It is imperative to connect with it and understand why certain events affected us so deeply. Connecting in a loving way will allow us to understand what is needed to heal.

Life is an inside job.

When the over-stimulated part feels our true desire to help and support, it will begin to *unfreeze*. We will find out what caused us to shut down and *split off* in the first place. From there we can change the programming and create what is needed to develop and become who and how we want to be.

The problem, until now, has been that we have not known how to make direct contact with our subconscious mind, to understand and know what is going on inside us at that level. With this work we can, in a safe and certain way, have direct contact with the part of our Self that carries the unprocessed events of our past. We put a stop to the looping of this unfinished business by reconnecting with these separated aspects of our Self. The more we collect these parts back, the more *whole* we become. This makes us more present and reestablishes our ability to choose. This is our power.

THE WORD TRAUMA

When we say the word *trauma*, most people think of it as something that happens when a person has been subjected to a devastating physical event or has been severely abused in some way. While these types of instant experiences can definitely be, and are, causes of trauma, it can also occur over a prolonged period of time without the experience of anything extreme happening physically or mentally.

In psychology, the terms *Big T and Little t* are used to differentiate the intensity of a traumatic experience. The DSM-5 (*Diagnostic and Statistical Manual of Mental Disorders*) defines a PTSD trauma as any situation where one's life or bodily integrity has been threatened. This would be a Big T trauma. A Big T trauma is one where we have been hurt or abused and we know it, like being in a car accident, experiencing war, being raped or severely abused or seeing someone hurt or killed. Any event that has had an obvious and significant emotional impact on us is a Big T.

A Little t can be a lot harder to spot because it is not overt or easily recognizable, and can be overlooked. They can occur from things such as:

- Living in a dysfunctional family dynamic.

- Being subjected to repeated mental or emotional abuse.

- Conflict with your children or siblings.

- Being bullied at school.

- Experiencing a divorce.

- Living with a high-functioning alcoholic.

- Having religious beliefs and/or ideologies forced upon us.

- Experiencing neglect as a child and/or not being seen or recognized.

- A child having any experience that overwhelms or confuses their undeveloped mind.

The Little t can be tricky because we do not realize the underlying messages being sent from the experience. For example, a high-functioning alcoholic unconsciously harbors feelings of self-loathing that can be subtly passed on to us. A mother's obsessive behavior is based on a deep fear of losing control, and her fearful energy can be subliminally placed within us. Someone living by stringent beliefs can pass them on to us and can, in effect, be teaching us not to trust ourselves and go against what we inwardly know to be right for us. A child who is not seen or recognized by their peers can develop feelings of separation, low self-worth, withdrawal or neediness.

Trauma comes in many different shapes, sizes and forms. In fact, trauma may not seem like the right word for everyone reading this book right now, but it is the only word we have in the English language that depicts *something stuck looping in the nervous system*. The effect of this looping comes out as a chronic condition or as a negative pattern. Trauma reveals itself in a myriad of ways, both large and small.

Some varying examples of how trauma reveals itself are:

- Dis-ease, addiction

- Chronic pain, weight or eating issues

- Anxiety or depression

- Attracting unhealthy or abusive relationships

- The inability to follow through in your job or career

- Self-sabotage of finances or success

- Feelings of low self worth and not being good enough

Whether a trauma is from a specific incident or caused over a prolonged period of time, the process for healing it is the same. Even if the cause of the negative pattern is unknown, the healing comes through accessing and *unfreezing* the unprocessed information that remains looping in the nervous system (NS).

The word trauma comes from the ancient Greek language and means *wound*. Originally it referred only to physical wounding, but today it refers to and includes mental and emotional wounding as well.

There are different ways that mental and emotional trauma occur, and we have different titles for them: *Developmental Trauma, Post-Traumatic Stress Disorder (PTSD), Complex PTSD, Acute Stress Disorder etc.* For now, though, for simplicity's sake, throughout this book we are going to call it all trauma, or *wounding*.

If you have an unwanted behavior or negative pattern and do not know where it stems from, that is okay. Through the process you will come to know the truth about why it is occurring. You will be given the ability to transform reactionary behavior coming from the past to a chosen response based in the present.

HOW WE PROCESS INFORMATION

The brain and the nervous system are incredibly complex parts of the body. The information given here has been generalized for ease of understanding in the context of this book. It does not go into the detailed individual functions of the brain, nervous system or the production of chemicals created in the body. This information has been simplified only to lead the reader to a clearer understanding about trauma, NTHP, and to instill a deeper sense of compassion within them while going through the process.

Let's start with the basics of how our brain handles incoming information—how it processes, deals with and stores our experiences. Information comes into our brain as unprocessed data from events and experiences that we encounter outside of us. This data is brought in through the right hemisphere of our brain, the part of the brain that deals with the creative and the formless. It is intuitive, imaginative and emotional. It takes in the overall picture and processes things like sound, color, imagery and sensation. The right brain then passes this information to the left hemisphere of our brain to make sense of it, understand it and file it away as experience for future reference.

The left brain deals with logic and understanding; it is analytical, driven to know and wants control. It is fact-based; it forms strategies and is detail-oriented. If an event, experience or situation is too frightening, too bizarre or outrageous to the point that it over stimulates the left brain, it may not be able to cope with and digest the information. If the left brain is not able to handle the event and it cannot be made sense of and filed, it will be rejected and shipped back to the right brain. What does the right brain do then? It does what it is supposed to do. It experiences the event again in its entirety—sees the overall picture with color, feels the sensations, hears the sounds and then sends it back to the left brain to be understood again. The left brain has another chance to deal with it, file it and put it to rest. If the information is still too much to accept, the left brain will reject it again and send it back to the right, only to be re-experienced and sent to the left again. The cycle has begun. The brain will continuously try to process the information and the looping of the experience becomes embedded in our nervous system. This looping event is considered to be trauma. It is like a record playing within us that is skipping over and over, with the needle cutting a deeper and deeper groove in the vinyl.

The brain's *modus operandi* is survival, so it will try and push this barrage of unwanted data out of the way; thus, it gets pushed into the subconscious. It is still very much alive and looping in the nervous system, trapped in the body as energy.

The event may be repressed, even forgotten over time, but the record is still playing in the recesses of our mind. We learn to either ignore it or compensate for it.

In my personal experience, I "forgot" the incidences of sexual abuse I experienced as a young boy. The events were so terribly confusing and painful for me that I managed to block them out of my mind. I completely suppressed them from my memory but, of course, they were not truly forgotten. After sixteen years of lying dormant to my conscious Self, the events awoke with great intensity. I was triggered by an emotional event that induced a similar emotion in me to what I felt as a child. I couldn't ignore the memory any longer. It was larger than life.

The event comes back to life when it is triggered by something that reminds us of the original experience. It can be a sound, a smell, an interaction with someone, or anything that simulates that original experience. This is when the volume on our record turns up high and we react to it. It plays the unwanted, overwhelming tune, and we experience the discomfort of the original event all over again, only this time it is coming out in our current experience.

Something stuck looping and unprocessed in the nervous system eventually has to out-picture itself in real time. What is going on within us mentally and emotionally is what we will experience in our outer world. This means the event circulating within us will come out as a negative pattern in our life, carrying with it the same energy and feeling as the original experience. When this happens, our past is having a dominating effect on our present life.

The Brain

LEFT

logic
RULES
CONTROL
RATIONALITY
objectivity
Analytic

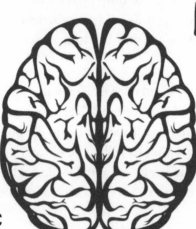

RIGHT

creativity
Sensational
Intuition
CURIOSITY art
Music

What Happens At The Time Of Trauma

Events first enter the right-brain as raw data.

The left brain processes and files the information.

But if the experience is too scary, outrageous, or overshelming for the left-brain to make sense of or understand **IT WILL REJECT IT...** then sends it back to the right-brain to be re-experienced. Thus starting the cycle of looping in the nervous system.

Looping Begins

Our right-brain uses the senses to experience what is happening in its entirety.

The right-brain sends the information to the left-brain to be made sense of.

When we go into trauma we **"Split Off"** from our present self and current reality.

If the left-brain continually fails to process:
* Time stops
* We split off
* We enter *fight or flight or freeze and immobility*

HOW TRAUMA IS ACTIVATED

Trauma occurs when our nervous system goes into a state of overwhelm, and we are unable to deal with the experience(s) or event(s) happening to us or around us. Why does this happen? The truth is, we do not fully understand why some people go into a state of trauma and some do not. In his book *Waking the Tiger,* Dr. Peter Levine gives examples of how, in a time of extreme distress, if a person stays moving physically and is focused on a purpose, it affects how their nervous system reacts, and they are less likely to go into the state of trauma. So, why do some stay conscious and in motion while others are thrown out of balance? There are just too many variables to say. But what we do know now is how trauma occurs and what happens to us.

When something is too scary, confusing or outrageous for our NS to bring to a reasonable understanding, the system breaks down in its ability to regulate itself. We experience a *shorting out,* as it were, because our NS is unable to cope with and process the event. This causes the experience to remain operating at the level of our mental, emotional Self. The reason for this is the NS, being the machine that it is, continues to try and process the information. The event continues to be cycled within us, going from the right brain (image/experience side) to the left brain (logic/control side) in the attempt to file it. We have to function in the world, so if this event or experience is too much for our left brain to handle, our brain pushes it out of the way, underground, out of our consciousness. The memory of the event stays looping at the "sub-" or "un-" conscious level, constantly going around and around like a skipping record within

"Without a solid and true foundation nothing will stay standing."

us, trying unsuccessfully to continue playing. In the meantime, we are left to cope with the mental and emotional effects of strife and dysfunction that come out of the event looping inside us.

What is happening to us at the mental/emotional level is cause to, and colors, how we perceive and experience events outside us. Until dealt with, the scenario that is looping un-processed in the subconscious mind will come out as some kind of negative pattern in our life.

The fact is, the vast majority of people in the world today are living with unprocessed experiences that are creating some form of dysfunction or chronic condition in their life. Most do not know why they have the condition or understand its workings. I will go so far as to say that **trauma is the most misunderstood, misdiagnosed and ignored dis-ease there is in the world today.**

OUR NERVOUS SYSTEM

I am sure most of you have heard the phrase: "The inside creates the outside." Let me explain as simply as possible how this is so; how our nervous system works in relation to trauma, and how what is going on inside us creates how we experience our outer world.

The NS is made up of the brain, the spinal cord and a large network of nerves that cover all parts of the body. Together, the NS helps different parts of our body communicate and allows our brain to control what is happening. The brain and the spinal cord make up what is called the *central nervous system.* The rest of the nerves together are called the *peripheral nervous system.*

Within the peripheral nervous system there are also two main sets of nerves: the autonomic nervous system and the somatic nervous system.

The *autonomic nervous system* is responsible for involuntary or unconscious functions of the body such as the beating of the heart, breathing, blinking, etc. The *somatic nervous system* is responsible for the voluntary control functions of the body that include movement, speech, chewing, etc.

There are two parts to the autonomic nervous system (ANS):

- The *sympathetic nervous system* activates and engages the body and allows us to function under stress. It is responsible for activities associated with the *fight or flight* response.

- The *parasympathetic nervous system* relaxes the body and has been called the *rest and digest, feed and breed* system of the body. It is associated with the *freeze and immobility* response.

*Even though these two parts are in constant opposition
to one another, a healthy ANS has the sympathetic and
parasympathetic continuously oscillating in a constant and
compatible manner that maintains a continuous harmony
and balance between the two.*

~ Karen Belfontaine MSW, RSW

The autonomic nervous system both stimulates and ultimately regulates the stress levels of the body. When our nervous system has been knocked out of alignment and fails to return to its regular rhythm of balance between the sympathetic and the parasympathetic, we go into the state of *fight or flight,* or *freeze and immobility.*

The first stage of trauma is *fight or flight.* However, when the *fight or flight* systems cannot be activated—when fighting our way out is not an option and escape is not possible or the traumatic threat is prolonged, the para-sympathetic branch of the autonomic nervous system is activated causing a state of *freeze and immobility.* Like a deer caught in the headlights, or an animal *playing possum,* freezing is a reflex—an instantaneous, instinctive response to a perceived threat. It is not a chosen action. Freezing can be the best way to ensure our survival.

If the ANS does not come back into balance, we will continue to experience one of these states long after the event is over, even when we are safe. The energy that comes from this experience is then what we are carrying inside us.

The information we have about energy and quantum mechanics shows us that whatever we observe or put our attention on, we affect. This means we become a part of the equation of what we are observing and that we are intangibly interacting with it. Therefore, the negative energy within us not only affects, but is actually a part of, what we are experiencing in our outer world. This internal energy wreaks havoc in our lives by impacting our interactions through its unconscious presence within us. We are recreating negative past events in our lives because inside of us they are still going on!

This is how the inside (the vibration of fear and anxiety that is being emitted through our nervous system) affects and skews how we experience outer events and circumstances. The inside creates the outside because this energy emitted from within us continues to replicate itself in our outer experiences—again and again and again...

Every human brain is both a broadcasting and receiving station.

~Napoleon Hill

We are now learning that the headquarters for the NS is the brain. This is where the pictured memory of the traumatic event lives and where the looping of the event (the battle of the sympathetic and the parasympathetic nervous systems) is perpetuated in consciousness.

A negative pattern operating in our life that we cannot consciously gain control of, is being caused by an overwhelming event from our past that is trying unsuccessfully to be processed. We can consider this reoccurring issue the universe's way of forcing us to pay attention to it. Realize that if we do not pursue it, it will pursue us. What I mean when I say that is, what is going on inside us will come out one way or another. If we do not do our inner work and heal the pattern, it will continue to come out in a negative way and over time can destroy our health, our relationships, our career ... or our life. On the other side of this, however, there is a great opportunity for the person who is willing to look inside and do their inner work.

WHAT HAPPENS WHEN WE ENTER THE STATE OF TRAUMA

Two things immediately occur when we enter the state of trauma: *time stops*, and we *split off*.

1) TIME STOPS

The event or experience continues to run within us, trying to be processed in present time. According to our subconscious mind, the incident is alive and still happening. It will reveal itself by attracting or creating experiences that will mirror the emotional equivalent of the initial event. They show up in our lives as negative patterns, such as anxiety attacks, anger, addiction, eating disorders, chronic pain, insomnia, etc. The pattern can also be of a more subtle nature, such as self-sabotaging, constantly going broke, or attracting abusive relationships. The bottom line is: if we have some form of negative, restrictive pattern that we have not been able to consciously change, we are guaranteed that it is because we have something stuck looping in our nervous system trying to be processed. We have all seen an adult, maybe even someone of status, have his/her buttons pushed and react like he/she was a child. Maybe that is exactly right, maybe they were triggered back to a time when an incident that carried that same energy occurred. When a trauma is triggered, we go back to that time.

2) WE SPLIT OFF

This means that the trauma has become its own separate entity, literally separated from our current and conscious Self. It circulates unconsciously of its own accord in our nervous system. We have heard the stories of people who have had a severe experience—an emergency room incident, a car crash or some other life-threatening event—who have left their body and watched the experience as if from above. They have *split off* from themselves. This is done out of survival, and because of the brain's need to preserve itself.

If this separation is so strong that the event looping in the subconscious becomes as real, or more real, than present-time reality, it falls under the category of schizophrenia, which simply means *split mind*. Schizophrenia has been given a severe connotation because of the extreme cases we have heard about or seen, but the truth is that many people have varying degrees of this separation going on within them. Because they are not aware of what is happening or how to handle it, they continue to live in, and have to deal with, this split state.

THE EFFECTS

A person responds to trauma in two different ways. As mentioned earlier, they will either go into *fight or flight*, or they will go into *freeze and immobility*. These are reflex responses that we have no choice about. We will first go into *fight or flight*, and it has been said that if we cannot get away, then we will go into *freeze and immobility*. There are many variables and unknowns as to what may influence the direction a person may go, far too many to be able to make any kind of sound conclusion as to why. Many things play a part in this: A person's genetic makeup, their character, the type of infraction they have encountered, and the timing, intensity and duration of the event all play a part. The exact same incident can have a completely different effect for different people. The commonality with trauma is that with both *fight or flight* and *freeze and immobility* responses, time stops, and the event continues to cycle in real time within the subconscious.

FIGHT OR FLIGHT

We all know someone, and can easily recognize the person who has gone into *fight or flight*. This person is the busy one, the one always doing something, always moving. Always busy doing, doing, doing. The irony is that our current society rewards this person for how hard they work and how much they accomplish.

In an extreme example, a person in *fight or flight* could be the director of a multi-million-dollar company—the person who has an insane work ethic and puts in long hours that no one else can, or is willing to do, that has driven him/her to the top of the corporate world. A person in *fight or flight* may also be the high-level athlete who pushes their body beyond its limits, going beyond normal boundaries, driven by a compulsion and a need they may not even understand.

Some high-profile athletes have come forward to share their stories of trauma. Like Major League Baseball player R.A. Dickey and Olympic gold medalist Kayla Harrison in *Sports Illustrated* magazine. They told their stories of childhood sexual abuse that kept them *running scared* for years, not letting them rest. Telling us that their "rise to the top," was not a fun one.

Not only do we see these people working themselves half to death trying to outrun their trauma, we see them celebrated for it! It can be very twisted and confusing for them. They are running from a fear that keeps them on a treadmill. They have an unconscious fear that if they stop they will feel and re-experience their trauma, be hurt, harmed or killed. This level of energy cannot go on forever, and most often they crash.

The *fight or flight* tapes that are continually running in a person are saying things like:

- Run!
- I have to get away!
- I can't stop!
- It's not safe. I have to go!
- I must keep moving!

FREEZE AND IMMOBILITY

The person who has gone into *freeze and immobility* is not always easy to spot. They may be the ones who avoid attention or confrontation and stay out of the limelight. They can be afraid of change and tend to stay in one place.

In an extreme example, this person could be a man living homeless on the street. He is frozen in time, locked into his response to the trauma he experienced. Very possibly, without even knowing he is doing it, he separates himself from engaging with the world in the hope that he will become invisible, thus safe from being hurt again. This instinct keeps looping in the subconscious mind of this person and, as we have learned, *out-pictures* itself in real time. They become frozen mentally and emotionally, which leads to the worst-case scenario of being physically immobilized. At this level, they are degraded in their ability to follow through or sustain any degree of accomplishment in their life.

The *freeze and immobility* tapes that continue to shut them down may go something like this:

- Don't look at/see me!
- I have to hide!
- Freeze!
- Don't move!
- I can't move!

Unaddressed, this will turn into "I can't" and "I'm not able" as core realities of their lives as the cycle progresses.

WHAT HAPPENED TO US HUMANS?

Most animals in the wild have a built-in system or ability that helps them deal with adversity, and to ultimately resolve the traumas they experience. Perhaps you have seen a bird fly into a window and fall to the ground as if it were dead. It lies there for a minute or two, gets up, gives itself a shake and then flies off. It is fine. It has released and let go of the trauma. Animals in the wild, like deer or antelope, may go in and out of potentially threatening experiences many times each day, but through their body's ability to process the information, they do not hold on to it or carry it around. It does not turn into trauma.

In his book *Waking the Tiger: Healing Trauma,* Peter Levine says that: "Most animals in the wild which experience a trauma through natural species interactions will go through a sequence of recovery stages. First, when the trauma or death is considered inevitable, the animal will 'faint,' losing sensory awareness and consciousness. If the trauma or death is averted, the animal will then partially waken out of that faint, and 'shake off' the trauma.

"This 'shaking off' looks remarkably like an epileptic fit, but when the movements are analyzed, they are a muscle-twitch repeat of the sequence of movements that animal took from the time it realized its hazard to the time it fainted. Once the 'shaking off' is complete, the animal is able to rise and continue its life activities without any longer-term impacts such as PTSD."

Neurologist Dr. Robert Scaer said: "Lasting trauma is only taken on when the 'victim' experiences repeated episodes of the same kind of helplessness and hopelessness. We humans are very good at giving ourselves and other species repeated episodes of helplessness and hopelessness, and animals which interact with us often pay a price in PTSD.

"In short, it is not the same disorder we as humans suffer from, as our brains are much more advanced and more of our brain is affected. Species of animals such as elephants and chimpanzees, found to have many social and neurobiological similarities with humans, have been found to suffer from this disorder."

The animals in the wild that do shake off the effects of trauma show an instinctive response that humans appear to lack. Did humans ever have this built-in system for releasing trauma? Perhaps, but it obviously has been lost over time. Maybe it happened as we evolved, as we had to worry less about predators and day-to-day survival. I do not know, but we clearly do not have it today, as a staggering number of people are walking around wounded, carrying unprocessed traumas that are creating dysfunction and wreaking havoc in their lives.

THE RETURN TO PEACE

The *Neuro Trauma Healing Process* will help us to tap into, *unfreeze* and give us the ability to re-program our thinking of the past. When I say *re-program*, I am not saying that we are to make up a new story about what happened to us. I am saying that we can *unfreeze*, release and give the energy back to that time, the time when it was happening. It is not actually happening anymore, and that energy creates an inaccurate response for the present. This allows us to return to our natural state of peace, calm, power and choice. In order for that to occur, we must first give our Self what we did not get at that time of the overwhelming event or experience. It could be the assurance of safety, love, acceptance or understanding that allows this to happen. Regardless, a higher level of trust must be created within us that allows the left brain to grasp the information that was once so outrageous. This causes the overall experience(s) to change. Only then can sense be made of it. It is at this point that the left brain can file it and put it to rest.

TRAUMA AND THE NEURO TRAUMA HEALING PROCESS (NTHP)

The *Neuro Trauma Healing Process* (NTHP) gives us safe and gentle access to the inner issue/experience and the ability to bring it to resolution. This happens by bringing the negative emotion back into conscious awareness in a safe and controlled way. Here it can be dealt with—seen from our current consciousness and perspective where healing automatically transpires.

Once we are conscious of what has been stuck and cycling inside us, we can connect with it. And we can then have the ability to recreate our response to what happened. A number of things occur when we have gained the ability to do this. One is that we create enough distance from the incident or feeling that we are not reacting to it anymore. It is not taking us over. This is very empowering, as we have reclaimed our right to choose. This puts us back in the driver's seat and back in control of our life.

It is important in the beginning that we work with a trained *NTHP* facilitator to help us *untangle*; that is, move far enough away from the experience so we can observe it and not be taken over by it mentally and emotionally. When this is possible, we gain what we call *traction*. *Traction* is when we have created a consistently safe, trusted and healthy connection to this life within us.

When this happens, the core programming has changed; therefore, so does the effect. Understand that this change occurs from the relationship created within us. It is within the process of connection itself where the healing occurs. When this inner relationship becomes positive and harmonious, we will then naturally and automatically start to have positive and harmonious experiences in our outer-world interactions. A synchronicity begins to reveal itself in our everyday events.

We have brought the event to resolution. From this place of awareness there is nothing left unprocessed to be triggered. The looping is no longer going on within our nervous system and therefore ceases to be recreated or *out-pictured* in our life. We will find ourselves free of the fear, anxiety, anger or the compulsion that has been occurring.

Only once this is fully established and the interaction with our Inner Self is consistently positive and healthy, and we can handle the things that come up safely, compassionately and confidently, can we take the work over ourselves. These wounded or confused parts of us will then be on the fast track to healing. (The time-frame is dependent on the person and circumstances, of course.) We then have the opportunity to develop and grow up normally, as we would have under safe and healthy circumstances.

When your inner world comes into order,
your outer world will come into order.

~ I Ching

UNDERSTANDING OUR NEED FOR LOVE

We humans are hardwired with a need for love. It is critical for us to be nurtured and to receive love. It is important to understand that everything we do—all actions we take, all decisions we make—are at their very core for the purpose of obtaining love or to keep ourselves from not being loved. This is not taken from Leo Buscaglia's love classes of the '60s though. Here is a sobering example…

In the 13th century, the German King, Frederick II, performed a horrible experiment. He wanted to discover what language a child would speak if they were never spoken to. Babies were taken from the loving care of their mothers at birth and put into the care of nurses. The nurses were instructed to look after the babies' basic needs of being fed and washed, and having their diapers changed. They were forbidden to talk to or touch the infants. Tragically, the experiment was stopped too late and the infants had died for want of love. There was no physiological cause for the deaths. The Italian historian Salimbene di Adam recorded the observation: "They could not live without petting." This horrific incident is evidence of how important love is to human survival. For infants, love is a necessity, a driving force behind all actions.

Anything that promotes feelings of love and intimacy is
healing; anything that promotes isolation, separation,
loneliness, loss, hostility, anger, cynicism, depression,
alienation, and related feelings often leads to suffering,
disease, and premature death from all causes.

~ Dr. Dean Ornish

This stage in our life, early childhood, is where the very foundation of our programming is set. It has been said that our basic persona is set by age five.

As infants, we adjusted our behavior to our environment and circumstances in order to secure love in our world. The unconscious decisions and con-clusions we made at such a young age may appear irrational and illogical to our current thinking. But when we realize that they were instinctual responses to what was actually a life-or-death situation, it makes perfect sense. We did the best we could, and we survived. Have compassion and admiration for this ingenious child. This compassion and admiration will be the key to *unfreezing* any trauma or negative pattern we hold. The patterns that developed while we were growing up continue to perpetuate into our adult life. Until they are brought into conscious awareness and addressed, this energetic pattern, this emotional need, will continue on into our current experience.

YOU ARE FUNDAMENTALLY GOOD!

At our very essence we are energy. At our most basic foundation we are a vibration. Simple grade-eleven science tells us this. It tells us that if we take any solid form and magnify it to the level of atoms and particles, we can see that it is not actually solid at all. An object may appear hard, like rock, metal, wood, plastic or a diamond, but if we were to magnify it we would see that all of these apparent solids are actually in a state of flux or circulation.

When we magnify these solids further, to the level of leptons and photons, we see that everything at its foundation—the petal of a rose, ocean coral, dust from the moon or human flesh and bone—have the same physical properties and are made up of the same carbon-based material. All matter has the same physical make-up at its foundation. If we magnify beyond that and consider the existence of quarks, we can accept that every apparent solid, including our physical bodies, are actually circulating energy, energy that is intelligent.

How is this relevant to trauma, you ask?

This is not a lesson in science, nor is it a religious statement. Please under-stand the relevance of the fact that at the core of our being is pure, intelligent energy. We can call it our source, our Authentic Self or higher power, but this energy inside us holds within it the expression of our energetic nature, the moving blueprint that is the very essence of our life. This intelligent energy is forever flowing out from our core to be expressed as our Authentic Self—our *Soul expression*.

This energy pushing out from our center carries with it our essential Self. It is, and always has been, available to us. Even though we may have had negative, possibly even atrocious, experiences, know that this pure positive energy at our core is not—and has never been—hurt or even damaged. It is still there, fully intact, fully available, waiting and willing to be expressed through us as us.

Through no fault of our own, both the way we have been treated and the way we have been made to feel have a direct influence on this articulation. Parents, teachers, siblings, ministers, etc. can influence us either positively or negatively. Whether they are well meaning or not, our reaction to their involvement in our life directly influences the delivery of this expression.

Positive influence creates a safe and natural pathway for our pure energy to flow through. It supports and nurtures our Authentic Self. Everything is aligned here, and inner conflict is not being created. Negative influence can alter, skew and even hold back our natural flow of energy, thus causing misalignment that, over time, will turn into some kind of dysfunction, negative pattern or even disease.

There is an epidemic in the world today. The vast majority of people have something wrong with them. **What is wrong with them? They *believe* there is something inherently wrong with them!** This may sound like a ridiculous comment, but it is at the crux of the human condition. It is untrue. You are fundamentally good. But if you, like so many others, believe that you are fundamentally flawed, then you stand in the way of the healthy and whole expression of *you*. For many people, this belief is cycling at the level of the subconscious and they are unaware of this programming that is sabotaging them, hurting them and stopping them.

The road to freedom and complete Self-expression starts when we begin to accept and embody these truths:

- I can heal from my past.

- My true Self (the pure, positive, intelligent energy at the core of my being) is fully intact, strong and capable.

- At the level of my Soul, I am not, and cannot be, permanently hurt or wounded.

- At my very core, I am whole and healthy.

If these truths feel foreign to you right now, and you find it hard to accept them, keep an open mind when doing this work. Let the process prove it to you.

Our Energetic Essence

Our Authentic Self - Our Soul
The core of our being that houses the blueprint of who we are.

At our very essence we are pure positve energy.
This energy is constantly pushing out from our center.

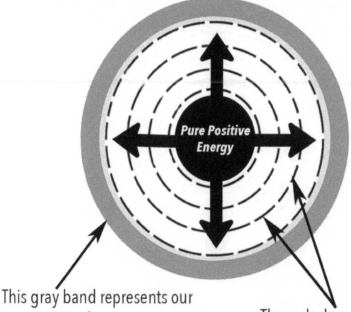

Pure Positive Energy

This gray band represents our **current conscious awareness.**

The white area inside this band represents what is operating at the level of the **sub-conscious mind.**

These dashes represent **positive and negative experiences** that have had an impact on our energy and who we have become.

How Our Energy Becomes
SKEWED

Negative influences out-picture in our life and can manifest as:
mental, emotional, and even physical pain, or lack of self-expression.

There are endless examples of negative life events that can store themselves
in our sub-conscious mind and form into erroneous beliefs and
detrimental patterns. When this happens our energy is negatively influenced
and the natural flow is inhibited.
It becomes - **SKEWED.**

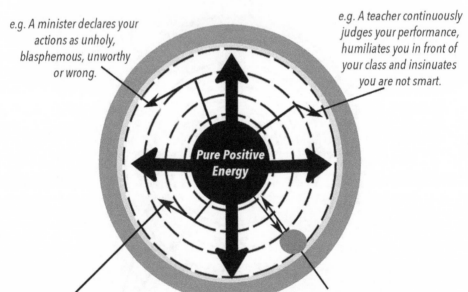

*e.g. A minister declares your
actions as unholy,
blasphemous, unworthy
or wrong.*

*e.g. A teacher continuously
judges your performance,
humiliates you in front of
your class and insinuates
you are not smart.*

**Pure Positive
Energy**

*e.g. A parent or sibling contiuously
puts you down and keeps you from
believing in yourself with words like:*
"You're not good enough",
"You Can't",
"You lack talent, looks, intelligence".

Toxic Shame
When we are abused as a child,
especially under the age of 5,
our energy is turned completely back in on iteself.
Blanket statements about our self form.
e.g. "I am bad", "I don't deserve",
"There is something wrong with me",
"I am not lovable".

"Toxic shame" is a term that was first coined by psychologist Silvan Tomkins in the 1960's. Unlike normal shame, toxic shame stays buried within the mind and becomes a part of our self-identity. In other words, a person suffering from toxic shame will experience a chronic sense of worthlessness, low self-esteem and self-loathing—all connected to the belief that they are innately "shameful" or "bad." **Toxic shame is the *internalized* and *buried* shame that rots within us.**

EXAMPLES OF NEGATIVE EXPERIENCES: COPING BEHAVIORS AND THEIR EFFECTS

Here are examples of what can happen when we experience, or are treated in ways that negatively impact us and separate us from our true and higher Self. These stories are examples of how incidences and programming can scar a person deeply enough to skew and even stop the natural course of a person's life.

These stories are universal and have been created to represent the challenges many people face. They do not represent any specific person.

ABUSIVE PARENT(S) - ALCOHOLISM

Arlene's father was a functioning alcoholic who would come home from work and get drunk most nights. His own upbringing was one of alcoholism, abuse and neglect. Arlene suffered through his constant verbal put-downs, his angry outbursts that seemed to come out of nowhere, and his snide remarks about her looks and intelligence. He made her feel worthless and unimportant, claiming she had a great life compared to what he'd had to endure. He was passing on to Arlene the same abuse he experienced as a child.

Coping behavior – Arlene desperately wanted her father's love and approval but was deeply wounded by his verbal put-downs and shaming. To cover up the hurt and anger she felt from his emotional blows, and the disappointment and despair she felt from not having the father she needed, she turned to the thing that was most readily available—alcohol. She withdrew from the outer world and drank to drown out her feelings; in effect, mirroring her father's own coping behavior and continuing the cycle of her lineage.

Effects – The effect this had on Arlene's adult life was an emotional and physical addiction to alcohol. In using alcohol as a tool to cover up her feelings of shame and anger, a pattern of involuntary self-medicating set in. She would attempt to avoid people and situations that would bring up unwanted feelings, but the more she drank, the more the feelings arose within her, until even everyday experiences became triggers. Arlene was out of control. Alcohol had taken her over and was poisoning all aspects of her life.

FORCED IDEOLOGIES - DEPRESSION

Mike grew up in a very religious family. Going to church was mandatory as long as he was living under his parent's roof. At a very young age he had been sent to an all-male religious school. According to his mother and father, guilt and self-sacrifice were demonstrations of pure devotion. Mike was made to feel unworthy of any achievements he made for himself. Whether his success was at school or on the sports field, he was taught that all glory was to go to God. Self-sacrifice was the only way to receive God's favor and to secure a place in heaven. It was seen as egotistical and a sin to feel good and show pride over an accomplishment and was punishable in the "eyes of God."

Coping behavior – Mike's coping behavior resulted from trying not to be judged by his parents, and by God. He suppressed any outward expression of happiness or joy for himself and gave all credit, glory and happiness to others and to God. He learned to put himself down immediately if he excelled in any way, countering the success he made with some other fault he possessed. This led to less and less outward expression. When he developed feelings of resentment and anger for not being allowed to strive to meet his full potential, he suppressed those feelings as well, believing they were the signs of weakness and a sin.

Effects – The effect this upbringing had on Mike as an adult was conflicting emotions, which eventually led to an inability to control them. He would have emotional outbursts of anger followed by deep feelings of shame, regret and remorse, which led to bouts of depression. He quit trying to excel, and this lack of drive had a negative effect on both his marriage and his work life. He was confused about why he had these emotions and did not know how to deal with them.

SEXUAL ABUSE - SHAME

Lori was eleven years old when a friend of the family sexually abused her. Her parents were helping out friends by letting their son stay with them while he went to college in their town. During that time, he was often entrusted to look after her and began to use these times as an opportunity to molest her. This happened numerous times. The events were not physically violent, but they were very manipulative. Lori was far too young to understand the complexities of what was happening to her. The abuse was the cause of great confusion because the perpetrator was affectionate and appeared to be caring. This made Lori feel good and important. She liked his attention but grew to realize that something was not right. Once he moved away and the abuse stopped, an overwhelming feeling began to grow in her that she was "bad" and had done something terribly wrong. She kept the abuse a secret and tried to block it out and erase it from her memory.

Coping behavior – Growing up, her feelings turned from confusion to shame. Lori unconsciously developed a coping behavior that would hide the fact that she was "bad." She did everything she could to appear "good." Lori became very busy, always moving and doing, doing, doing. She excelled as a runner and entered marathons. She joined many extracurricular groups and activities that kept her busy and occupied. Staying busy didn't allow her the time or space to have any intimate relationships and all of her male friends were just acquaintances.

Effects – The effect this abuse had on Lori's life was a deeply-seated confusion over her sexuality; she was cold and was mistrustful of relation-ships. She became out of touch with her true feelings and therefore her inner guidance system, making her a poor judge of character. This led to many dramatic experiences and some unhealthy relationship choices. Her profession became a means of escape and her excuse for not having time for an intimate relationship. Lori created a world where she was too busy to think about the dysfunction she felt. It was as if her life had been turned into a treadmill of busyness. She would push herself to the point of exhaustion and burnout but could not stop. She was physically, mentally and spiritually drained.

THE EXPERIENCE OF WAR - OVERWHELM

Ron was sent overseas to serve as a soldier for his country. He was just twenty-one and freshly drafted into the army. Three months into his tour of duty he was sent into combat. His squadron was unexpectedly ambushed, and his troop was hit hard. It was a horrific scene with explosions, gunfire and panic. Many of his comrades were killed or wounded. His best friend, with whom he went through training, lost his legs in an explosion right before Ron's eyes. Miraculously, Ron survived physically unscathed, but the sight, sound and smell of death and fear filled his head and mind and would not leave.

Upon his return home, Ron had long bouts of insomnia. When he was able to sleep he experienced terrible nightmares. Lack of sleep led to irritation in his waking hours and a re-experiencing of the event over and over in his mind. He was on edge all the time and felt out of place, as if there was something wrong with him. He felt he was not a participant in life, as if he was outside of situations—watching. He was unable to relax. He thought: "I must be going crazy."

Coping behavior – In a short period of time, Ron knew he could not cope and that he needed help. He knew he could not handle suffering any longer. He saw a doctor who sent him to a psychiatrist who put him on anti-depressant medication for the daytime and sleeping pills for the night.

Effects – While the medications gave him some immediate relief, Ron soon began to have side effects. Emotional breakdowns and paranoia would set in randomly and without warning, sometimes in inappropriate places and times. This was not like Ron at all, and the lack of command over his emotions was humiliating to him. Thoughts of suicide began to creep in. The doctors wanted to give him another medication for this. Ron felt like he was losing control of his life, like it was no longer his own.

FINANCIAL LACK - LOW SELF-WORTH

Emily's parents were the sweetest people you could imagine. They were very caring, loving people and an integral part of Emily's life. They had the best of intentions and loved her deeply. However, her parents grew up during the Great Depression, and carried an attitude of *never having enough*. This attitude held a great amount of fear around money and its scarcity. It carried with it an inability to have or get what they needed and wanted. Often, they would tell Emily: "We cannot afford it … it's too good for us … you really don't need that." Through school Emily either wore clothes made by her mother or bought from a second-hand or thrift store. Everything the family purchased was from some kind of discount center. Her father always worked full time and made a reasonable wage, but they were afraid to spend money if it wasn't absolutely necessary. Going to the fair once a year was a big treat. All other entertainment came from Emily's imagination and what she could find to play with in their home.

Coping behavior – Emily became quite creative in her early years. She learned to sew and bake, and she became quite talented at arts and crafts. To try and fit in with her classmates, Emily made herself new clothes from excess material her mother had. She was extremely polite and always used the best manners. Her motivation came from the underlying feeling that she was inferior and less deserving than others.

Effects – In her adult years, Emily became acutely aware of her feelings of inadequacy and *not enough*. This showed up in her finances and in expectations of people in her life. She would automatically put herself beneath others and therefore be treated as such. Even if her qualifications at work out-shone her co-workers, she felt *less than* and undeserving. Financially, she could never seem to get above a certain level of savings. Whenever there was a surplus, something would inevitably happen to bring her back to the same level of scarcity she grew up with. She rarely felt secure, only ever having enough to meet her needs. When it came time to buy new things or, heaven forbid, go on a vacation, she was too afraid to spend the money, so most times she didn't. The more time went on, the more it felt like the walls were closing in on Emily. She felt trapped in a very small and restrictive world.

Conclusion

These stories are examples of how incidences and programming can skew and even stop the natural course of a person's life. The people in these stories experienced something that could scar them for life. Unaddressed, these negative patterns would continue to cycle inside of them, creating dysfunctional behaviors and experiences. It is imperative to access the

You cannot heal fear by fearful means or avoidance.
~ Unknown

wounding(s) and bring it to resolution in order for the pattern to discontinue. Once this occurs, the person has the freedom to choose in the present moment and stop the past from running the show.

The Effects Of Trauma

Physical Health
Disease in the Body
Chronic Sickness or Pain
Lack of Energy or Drive
Obesity or Eating Issues
Insomnia

Mental, Emotional & Spiritual
Poor Self Esteem or Lack of Confidence
Feeling Disconnected or "Cut Off"
Feeling Unheard or Unseen
Substance Abuse
Depression or Anxiety
Loss of Imagination or Play

Relationships
Attracting Unhealthy Relationships
Emotional & Physical Abuse
Poor Communication
Feeling Unworthy or Unloveable
Lack of Self Expression

Success & Achievement
Lack of Purpose
Difficulty Following Through
Lack of Clarity or Direction
Continual Self Sabotage
Always Falling Short
Not Being Enough
Financial Issues

SUSTAINABLE HEALING

Understand that you can do all the right things, take all the correct steps, get the right education, work hard, do things the right way, and even try to think right, but it will not be enough. As long as the tapes continually running within you are telling you things like "I can't … There's something wrong with me … I'm not smart enough … I don't deserve … Nobody sees me … I'm not likeable—or loveable …" they will taint your abilities and depict the experiences you have in your outer world, no matter what you do.

How can you expect any sustainable healing, health or success with recordings like these constantly playing inside you? Think of a fish swimming upstream against the current, trying to get to the calmness of a lake ahead. If he stops swimming while in the current, he will be pulled back down the river he just swam up. So, too, will it be with someone who does not do their inner work. They will be continuously fighting against a current of negative thoughts and feelings that keep them stuck and pull them back. The subconscious mind is much more powerful than the conscious mind. To continually fight against this current is a very hard way to go through life. So, how do we stop this vicious cycle? How do we stop struggling and fighting our way through life? How do we reach the lake? The first step is to understand what is going on in our subconscious mind. Earl Nightingale said: "Whatever we plant in our subconscious mind and nourish with repetition and emotion will one day become reality." And let me clarify, it doesn't matter if it's positive or negative. Anything that is cycling within our subconscious is being *nourished* and will come out as our reality.

Whatever we plant in our subconscious mind and nourish with repetition and emotion will one day become reality.
~ Earl Nightingale

CORE BELIEFS

The worst-case scenario of becoming disconnected from our Authentic Self comes from negative incidences that happened to us before the age of five. The reason for this is: at this early age, the instinct to do anything that is necessary to receive love and care is incredibly strong. As we saw in the experiment with the babies, it is a life or death situation. At that age, our parents are our only source and supply of everything, including that which sustains our life. As an infant, who fed us? Who protected us? Who nurtured and looked after us? Hopefully, our parents did. As an infant our parents or main caregivers are everything to us—they virtually become God in our eyes. This tainted idea of our parents *as our source* is what so many have unconsciously carried with them into adulthood. This idea comes with all the flaws, dysfunctions and shortcomings of our parents, because our model is based on the false idea that our parents are *God/Source*! This is an enormous issue that remains intact within many people into their adult life without their realizing it. This is a key to understanding where our core beliefs about God, Allah, Buddha, Higher Self, The Universe, etc. stem from. If we look at this with open eyes we may see that our relationship with this spiritual entity actually mirrors our relationship with our parents.

The infant mind cannot conceive of the idea that her parents, or the adults who sustain her, could be wrong in any way. To make them wrong would cause the child's whole world to implode. The child then comes to the conclusion that: "It cannot be them ... so it must be me."

This is why abuse or neglect at this stage is so very damaging. What is fed to an infant is trusted as truth. When you love an infant, being deserving of love becomes their truth. Abuse an infant, and being deserving of abuse becomes their truth. This is where core beliefs like: "I'm no good ... I'm a bad person ... I don't deserve ... I can't," and "there's something wrong with me" come from. Core beliefs such as these attract relationships that mirror our parental programming and color every aspect of our present life. In the 1960's, psychologist Silvan Tomkins coined this as *toxic shame*: core, shameful beliefs about ourselves that have become blanket statements of who we wrongly perceive ourselves to be. These beliefs cast a black cloud over anything and everything we try to do in our life. As an infant or child, these beliefs not only block the energy from our Authentic Self from flowing outward, they also send the energy back inward denying *who* and *what* we really are: loveable, deserving, intelligent, powerful and creative.

WHAT WE DO

We do a variety of things to try and make up for the limiting beliefs and feelings we have about ourselves. We try to overcome, we cope, we compensate, we settle.

WE TRY TO OVERCOME

We try to overcome the limiting beliefs and behaviors by doing more, working harder, accomplishing and persisting. Primarily, this is a masculine and a *fight or flight* trait. It tends to be seen as a positive characteristic in our society. Praise is received for hard work and accomplishments, but when overcoming is done to cover up a perceived or potential shortcoming, it is a façade that is very hard on us. Most times, sustaining the degree of energy required to keep up the façade is impossible, because the façade is out of alignment with what is really happening inside us. It is out of alignment with our Authentic Self and does not allow our energy to flow naturally. The need to stay intensely alert and *on top of our Self* leads to fatigue, frustration and burnout. Breakdowns occur when we are unable to keep the façade up any longer and the blocked energy spills out or boils over as we *break down* or *lose it* in some way.

WE COPE

We cope with our limitations and shortcomings out of necessity. Coping is a means of survival, *not* coping feels like we are giving up. Our sense of survival pushes us to do what it takes to *stay afloat, stay alive, stay on top* or whatever the case may be. There is nothing wrong with coping, until it is not enough anymore. Simply coping is fear-based and prevents us from living to our highest and truest potential.

Most of the help that is taught and given to people through mainstream therapy are ways to cope. Very few of them address how to bring the issue to resolution; that is, to heal it for good. I am not discrediting any program or system, but the fact is, we are evolving and so is our ability to heal.

WE COMPENSATE

The truth is, most of us live lives of compensation, either consciously or unconsciously, to varying degrees. We want to be the best we can, and therefore we want to improve our *shortcomings* by being diligent in that area. We compensate for what we feel we lack or are not good at. We compensate in a number of ways. We have all seen the person who tries to make himself/herself out to be more successful, more intelligent and more impressive than they actually are. Someone who does not feel like he is worthy or valuable may boast about how successful he is in the hope that others will believe and accept him.

The core beliefs I personally carried within me were: "I'm a bad person, I've done something wrong." When I discovered that this was how I felt in the deepest part of my being, it absolutely rocked me; I did not know what to make of it. Over time, I started to see why I had become such a *nice guy*. How often I heard the comment of *what a nice guy* I was. My compensation for feeling like I was a bad person was to make everyone think I was a really nice guy. This happened unconsciously, and as I became aware of this belief I could see my compensation loud and clear.

WE SETTLE

We can appear very noble in our explanations of why we settle for less than we want and deserve. We can tell ourselves that: "I'm doing fine just the way I am," or, "Others have it much worse." Both of these statements may be true and may even feel empowering, but if we have beliefs running within us that are saying: "I can't," or, "I don't deserve," then these statements are lies that keep us from stepping out and living our life. Our fear of being shut down or hurt, like we were in the past, is preventing us from living to our fullest potential. This way of living can appear to be honest and noble, but in actuality is very restricting, unfulfilling and is going against what is trying to happen—becoming who we really are.

We can try to push through these beliefs and events that keep us stuck doing the same thing over and over. We can compensate and act like something we are not. We can try to settle and accept our fate. Or we can do our inner work with the *NTHP* and bring these issues to a full and complete resolution. We can regain our peace of mind and allow our life force to flow freely through us.

Congratulations on choosing the latter. You are now on the fast track to living the life you came here—and deserve—to live.

Until you make the unconscious conscious,
it will direct your life and you will call it fate.

~ Carl Jung

BECOMING OUR OWN SOURCE

Through the *Neuro Trauma Healing Process*, we are able to identify, understand and dissolve the blocks, allowing our natural energy to flow unrestricted. By doing this we bring forth the expression and gift of who we really are. When we are free of the blocks and our energy is flowing unbound, we naturally become our own source of acceptance, safety, security and love. Thus, this is what comes back to us from the world.

We will see that in reality we cannot receive from outside of ourselves that which we do not give our Self within. As we do this process and learn how to love ourselves, we will see the things we have desired coming to us naturally and easily, as if by magic. We will begin to understand why we have been receiving what we have, and why it is a perfect vibrational match to what we have been thinking and believing subconsciously. As we realize this, we are able to take over more *response-ability*. We are no longer reacting from our past, we are becoming more present and at choice. From this place we have the keys to our life back and can be in the driver's seat, perhaps for the very first time.

So far in this book, very little has been mentioned about the positive support and encouragement that enhances the energy flowing from our Authentic Self. This is because this programming supports us and is not in our way. Just as we have negative, energy-stopping people and experiences, so too, do we have ones that have helped us to move forward. Be clear though, at some point even someone who enjoyed wonderful parents and a supportive upbringing will need to become their own source as well. It seems this is the way the game of life is set up. Eventually, we all have to take responsibility for our life and become our own source of safety, fulfillment and love.

As we bring into consciousness the events that have been unconsciously running us, we develop the ability to take control of our life. We have another chance. We have an opportunity to give our Self a new program that is in alignment with our blueprint—our Soul.

When our conscious and subconscious minds are aligned and in agreement, there is nothing in our way and what we desire will become manifest in our life.

MEDICATIONS: YOU CANNOT HEAL WHAT YOU CANNOT FEEL

Everybody wants to be healed, happy and successful, but in our current society we have been sold a misleading bill of goods. We are being told that behavioral medications can *fix* us when we do not feel well or happy! While this is a generalization, the fact is, the pharmaceutical industry is flourishing and their marketing is visibly influencing and having a dominating effect on many lives.

There is, in my opinion, a proper time and place for anti-depressant and behavioral medications. If you are dealing with an intense or dangerous psychological condition where you pose a danger to yourself or others, or if you are having trouble functioning and are using them temporarily to get through a very tough time, then they can be warranted and helpful. However, very few people need to be on the *meds for life* program that has become so common today.

Anti-depressants are prescribed to make people feel better, but they do this by masking the root cause of their pain. It is astounding how successfully these medications are in their ability to completely block out a person's true feelings. Medications make it very difficult for a person to recognize what is truly going on inside them at the emotional level. The saying "The healing is in the feeling" has a lot of truth to it. Behavioral medications tend to be a *Band-Aid* solution that keeps people from feeling, and therefore from any real and lasting healing. I have worked with many people who were taking medications. Most of these people, after going through the *NTHP* process, no longer need them and are now medication free.

Since these drugs mask your true feelings, they tend to slow down the process of this work. While doing this work on medication, it will probably take you more time to sort through what is actually real or true for you before you can reach the heart of the matter. It is more difficult, but if you persist, the process cannot help but work. The time-frame for healing varies depending on the person, the type of drug and the prescribed amounts, but rest assured you can get there. The *NTHP* process will guide you in your goal of becoming healthy and ultimately medication-free.

You will find that as you heal and create inner harmony, you will want and need to be medicated less and less. The aim is to resolve the root cause of your anxiety, fear and stress, not to bury it. When this resolution happens, you will feel safely in tune with what you are feeling, and you will be able to trust your emotional compass again.

If you are on anti-depressants or any kind of behavioral drug right now and would like to do the *Neuro Trauma Healing Process*, **I advise not ending their use abruptly. If being medication-free is your goal, consult your doctor and work with him/her to slowly wean yourself off the medications.**

A GREAT STORY-YOURS

It takes a great amount of bravery to take responsibility for your life and investigate the forces that appear to be working against you.

As you heal your past, believe it or not your past will become a healthy part of your life. Once you are no longer run by the effects of a painful past, you will be able to see just how far you have come, and who you are without that anchor. It is the story of what brought you here today, and the process of awakening and becoming free.

In James Hillman's book, *The Souls Code: In Search of Character and Calling*, he tells people's stories of challenging upbringings that drove them to create great outward success in their life. I applaud those who find a way to use their negative experiences to a positive result. Unfortunately, there are also countless examples of people who have reached great outer achievement and are seen as successful, but who are in actuality desperately unhappy. Hearing the news of comedian Robin Williams taking his life affected me deeply. To see someone so caring, funny and so loved by millions take his own life—someone who seemed to have it all but who was actually so deeply unhappy and disturbed, seemed very wrong. He is just one of the many examples of entertainers, athletes and business moguls who have reached the pinnacle of outer success—who appeared to have it all, only to destroy themselves through drugs or alcohol and ruin or take their own lives. These mental-illness effects are driven by the inability to cope with what is going on inside of them.

I am not minimizing the accomplishments of these people in any way, quite the contrary, but you are evolving and do not need to be driven by the negative experiences of your past to this degree any longer. You can now achieve success from a place of peace and understanding. Instead of fighting against your past, you will be able to understand it, harness it and use the energy in the positive way I believe it was intended.

True success comes from a place of peace and inspiration, not out of a need to prove or redeem yourself. This is a much more secure way to live and does not carry with it the repercussions of battling against your past. It is the path of least resistance that comes out of wholeness. **It is a path based in security and certainty that allows your natural Self to flow out with a sense of joy.**

Client Testimonial:

*Through the **NTHP** process I was helped to understand why I hold on to feelings so much and how it can hurt to do so. I went on a journey through past, deep-rooted, unfinished business … I learned to forgive, let go and accept events that are a part of my life in a loving and understanding manner. I now embrace the flow of life and feel more confident and responsible about my decisions.*

Part 2

THE PROCESS

This guidebook is written in 2nd person narrative so that it will read more personally and clearly to the reader. Facilitators in training can use this book and change the perspective for working with a client.

*In order to be qualified to facilitate this process for others, you must have full Certification through AEL - *An Extraordinary Life.*

Everyone can benefit from this process, but it seems that the people most in need are those who have trauma, chronic conditions or addiction running and ruining their life. This book was written with those people in mind, and for the counselors, coaches and therapists who will be facilitating them through their healing.

As mentioned earlier in this book, *the inside creates the outside,* and to become a facilitator of this work this principal firmly applies. It is important to understand that if you want to be a facilitator of *NTHP,* the information and process in this book are not just standard learning, they are standard healing for you, personally, first. You must collect the separated parts of your Self back, heal your fragmentation and become *whole* before it will be possible for you to facilitate someone else beyond their fragmentation. It is as simple and straightforward as that.

If you are not healed and in alignment personally, it is possible you will be triggered in your life or through your experiences with your client. So, the process of becoming an *NTHP* facilitator first begins by fully going through the process and doing the work yourself. It is a beautiful thing: in order to be an effective facilitator, you need to first be healed and whole yourself. Knowledge means very little, it is the practical experience of healing and becoming whole that makes us an effective conduit. Being an *NTHP* facilitator is not just about being a messenger of information, but an opening for others of the living message.

BEFORE EMBARKING ON THIS WORK

Please, do not think you have to do this work alone. Everyone needs help in the beginning. Going it alone, you may be able to make the internal connection, but understand that, because we are looking through the filters of our own experience, we can only take ourselves so far.

The beauty of it is: you can take this work over yourself once you have gained *traction* and have created a consistently positive and healthy connection to your Inner Self. You will then have first-hand experience and understanding of the workings of the subconscious mind.

> *For safety and effectiveness, we encourage you to work with a trained* **NTHP** *facilitator to initiate this process.*

> *There are on-line facilitators we can set you up with that can help you wherever you are. Please take advantage of them. www.reclaimyourpowerprocess.com*

- **If you are on behavioral medication,** we recommend that you consult with your doctor before beginning this work.

- **If you are currently seeing a counselor or therapist,** you may want to consult with them before embarking on this journey.

- **If you are a therapist or counselor,** first of all, congratulations, and thank you for reading this book. I hope that through this book you will understand and experience how powerful and needed this work is. *NTHP* reveals to people their innate power to fully heal from their past, something that has not been previously available. We need more people trained to facilitate this work. Please know that our door at *An Extraordinary Life* is always open to you.

HOW THE PROCESS WORKS

As the title says, this work is process driven—the exercises are intertwined with one leading directly into the other. These three steps create the process that gives you direct access to your subconscious mind.

1. The *Snapshot*

2. The *Compassionate Letter*

3. *Connection and Relationship*

They need to be done in the order presented with no gap in between; one right after the other with no lapse. If not done this way, the process will not work. Make sure you have at least one hour of uninterrupted time to do each step to completion. Be good to, and honor yourself. Do not shortchange yourself by rushing through it or by only doing a part of it at a time. One hour should be enough but give yourself whatever timeframe is necessary for you to feel complete with each step. Be sure to give yourself some extra time afterward to rest so things can sink in and your body can recalibrate.

The more fully you commit to allowing the process to follow its course, the more effective it will be. This means: giving the feelings or emotions that arise the permission and space they need to be felt and listened to without judgment. That being said, please do not do anything you are not comfortable doing or go to an emotional place that does not feel safe to you. When I take my clients through this exercise, I tell them: "You don't have to do anything you don't want to do" and "You are always in charge." Even if you are further advanced, have already done the initial exercises and are writing on your own, it is always good to instill this affirmation of security in yourself. This is how you start learning to check in, to feel within yourself and to trust the feeling.

Remember, you are not here to break through or overcome anything. You are here to create a safe and compassionate connection to the life within you.

That is the biggest breakthrough you can have. It is also where the healing actually occurs. Forcing something out or pushing through something will just create more mistrust, fear and even deeper withdrawal. Trust me, this is the voice of experience speaking here. For this exercise, **set the intention to be kind to yourself and to create a safe and compassionate connection to that within you**. That is your goal.

WHAT YOU WILL NEED IS:

- A quiet and private space.

- No distractions: turn off all phones, radio, TV or anything that will distract or interrupt you.

- At least one hour of uninterrupted time.

- A pen or pencil and plenty of paper (lined, preferably).

- To do the series of three exercises one after the other, each one to completion.

- To keep yourself hydrated. (The work you are about to do is left/right-brain work that will reach parts that may not have been accessed in quite some time. The effect is a literal workout for your brain, so drink water, herbal tea or some kind of hydrating drink. Stay away from caffeine, alcohol or beverages high in sugar.)

- Time afterwards to rest, 15–30 minutes.

LET'S BEGIN!

The process itself is very simple and easy. As long as you keep an open mind and follow the exercises as they are outlined, there is nothing more to know. You will simply be taken to where you need to go. Do the following exercises and let the process guide you.

We are now ready to begin the *Neuro Trauma Healing Process*, starting with the *snapshot*. **First, read through the directions of how to write your** *snapshot* entirely and find out what type of *snapshot* fits your situation, and write it directly after that.

1) THE SNAPSHOT

The *snapshot* is a description of an emotionally charged past event or experience that has resulted in a negative pattern or chronic condition in your life. It is most effective to use the earliest experience or event possible. If you suffered a childhood trauma, use it, even if you think you have already dealt with it. I can assure you that it still holds negative energy and can be the cause of many of the current issues you are experiencing. Sometimes there is no memory of a disturbance. A *snapshot* can also be a description of an unwanted pattern or behavior in your life of which you do not know the origin. Either way, it is important to go back to the earliest possible recollection or experience of it. The *snapshot* is to be written in such a way that if someone else were to read it, they would completely understand what happened or happens to you and have compassion for you. It is not an emotional outpouring, but a factual account, according to you. You are not trying to fix anything with this *snapshot*, just explain the, *who, what, when, where* and *how* of it. Do not hold anything back.

This is the part of the process that will give us the *emotional in* required to access the subconscious mind.

Be on your side and be good to yourself.

Write your *snapshot* in the form of a story. Be sure to include how you felt at the time. Go into as much detail as you can but remember: it is up to you to keep yourself safe. Do not go into an emotional place you are too uncomfortable with, or do not know how to handle.

Important to Note:

You are safe to speak the truth here. No one will read this *snapshot*. Do not hold anything back. Do not worry about protecting anyone, or about being spiritually, politically or historically correct. Just do the best you can. Nor do you need to be concerned with looking like a victim. Just say it like it is without defending other's actions or minimizing the experience(s). Put down on the page what happened the way you remember it.

THE BASICS INSTRUCTIONS:

- Your *snapshot* must be handwritten. Do not use a keyboard or typewriter.

- Write a minimum of half a page to a maximum of a full page. Make sure it is complete with as much detail as you can recall.

- Write it in the native language you grew up with or that you used at the time.

- Do not worry about neatness or grammar, as long as you can read it.

- Refer to yourself in first person, i.e.: "I felt…"

- Write as if you are writing to someone else describing the story of what happened to you.

- Remember, it is not an emotional outpouring but a description of the facts as you recall them.

- Reach for the earliest memory or experience. The further back you go the easier and more powerful this exercise will be for you. It should bring you back to the recollection, and ultimately the feeling of the experience.

- Tell it like you recall it. **Be on your side.**

HOW TO WRITE YOUR SNAPSHOT

There are four different types of snapshots: You will recognize which one pertains to you. There are specific details and examples listed further below.

- Snapshot for a specific or *known trauma*.

- Snapshot for a *chronic condition with an unknown origin*. (Something that physically affects the body: obesity, depression, chronic pain, etc.)

- Snapshot for a *negative pattern with an unknown cause*. (An intangible: self-sabotage, lack, continually hitting a financial ceiling, attracting abusive relationships, etc.)

- Snapshot for a *long-term scenario that you suspect is the cause of dysfunction in your life*. (A dysfunctional family dynamic, forced religious beliefs, etc.)

FOR A SPECIFIC OR KNOWN TRAUMA

– This *snapshot* is for any "Big T" Trauma. Follow *the basic instructions*, and be sure to include:

- Pertinent events that led up to the trauma.

- Anyone else involved or pertinent to the story.

- Details of the experience.

- How you were affected at the time. How you felt and acted.

- Clarity and enough description to bring you back to the feelings and emotion you experienced.

Sample Snapshot for a Known Trauma:

I was six years old when my mother contracted a debilitating disease that put her into the hospital and kept her there, bedridden for a two-year period. My father's job kept him working most evenings, and so he asked my older cousins to babysit my brother, Chris, and me after school. Chris was four years older than me and often was off with his friends. My one cousin, Brett (who was eighteen) looked after us two or three times a week. Being a little girl, I idolized and, dare I say, fell in love with Brett. He paid a lot of attention to me and made me feel important and cared about. After a couple of months he began to take me into the bedroom or out in the forest behind our home. At first he just touched me; it felt okay, and I enjoyed being paid so much attention. He made me feel special, and I liked it; it felt like affection. But then it escalated to him rubbing against me and eventually trying to penetrate me. I knew something was not right, I felt confused and somehow dirty. I wanted his attention so badly and didn't want to upset him, so I would let myself be talked into it. I can still feel how sad I was when he would get angry when I didn't want him to touch me, and how conflicted I was when it hurt me physically. I started wetting the bed and having nightmares. I wanted the molesting to stop, but I still wanted him to like me. I was afraid he would be angry with me, though, and I would lose his "love." He told me that if I told anyone about this, it would make my mom even sicker, and then she might never come home again. I felt so alone and confused about the secret. This went on for the whole time my mother was in the hospital.

FOR A CHRONIC CONDITION WITH NO KNOWN ORIGIN

– Follow *the basic instructions* on how to write a *snapshot* along with these considerations.

If you have a chronic condition in your life that you want to heal but you do not recall or know of any traumatic experience as the cause, you will need to describe a time when the condition took hold of you with great emotion or energy and when it was at its worst. Describe in detail what happened and how it made you feel. Have the *snapshot* be clear and descriptive enough to bring you back to the feelings you experienced, and have compassion for yourself at that time. Go back to the earliest recollection of an extreme time. If you use something recent, i.e., last month or even last year, you will likely find it hard to create enough separation from the event.

Sample Snapshot for a Chronic Condition:

It was about ten years ago that I realized I had a serious issue with pain. I was only thirty-four years old and I looked like I was in good health, but I wasn't. I had extreme joint pain. I was on a business trip and got stuck in the airport due to a snowstorm. All of the hotels in the city were booked up, and we had to stay overnight in the airport boarding area. It was very uncomfortable with no soft place to lie down, and the pain medication I was using seemed to be having less and less of an effect as time went on. The pain eventually flared up to the point where my whole body was throbbing. I couldn't get comfortable, and when I went to get up or walk, it escalated to an unbearable pain in my lower legs and ankles.

I got very frustrated, because I knew that if I didn't move it would become even worse. I got really angry with myself for needing to ask for help, because I could not even stand up on my own. I was getting looks from people in the airport that made me feel embarrassed and humiliated. It made me feel as if I was being a whiner; no one understood. I felt completely trapped in the pain of my own body. There was no escape, and I couldn't move to get out even if there had been a way. I felt hopeless and helpless.

FOR AN INTANGIBLE NEGATIVE PATTERN

– Follow *the basic instructions* on how to write a *snapshot* along with these considerations.

Write this *snapshot* if you have a negative intangible pattern in your life (self-sabotage, attracting unhealthy relationships, lack, etc.) that you want to heal but do not recall any traumatic experience taking place. You will need to pick the most emotionally charged memory you have of this reoccurring pattern. What I mean is: recall a time when you experienced the pattern and it felt so strong that it continues to bring up emotion in you now when you think of it (it may currently be coming up as flashes of memory or emotion for you). Have the *snapshot* be clear and descriptive enough to bring you back to the feelings and emotions you experienced to the point of having compassion for yourself at that time.

Sample Snapshot for a Negative Pattern:

I was out to dinner with a woman I had recently met. I really liked her. We had hit it off right away when we met two weeks earlier. We had been talking a lot on the phone since then. We were both very happy and excited to get together. It felt like a Soul connection.

We had a very nice dinner at a dimly lit Greek restaurant. After the meal, the waitress came over to take payment. I gave her my debit card only to be told it was declined. I felt panic. I knew I had enough money in my bank account to cover this. I was devastated and didn't know what to do because I knew my credit card was maxed out, too. I desperately gave it to the waitress anyway. And, of course, this was declined as well. I felt completely humiliated asking if they would take a check (they did not).

My date ended up paying for the dinner. I was mortified. She was quite taken aback by the events too. I felt so dark and like a complete loser. I have struggled financially for most of my life. Something always keeps me from getting ahead. It turned out this time that the government had taken money directly out of my account without my knowing, to pay overdue income tax. Needless to say, I never went out with that woman again ... I feel like there is something working against me, and I just can't win!

FOR A LONG-TERM SCENARIO

– Follow *the basic instructions* on how to write a *snapshot* along with these considerations.

This *snapshot* is about the way you were treated in a certain environment and how that dynamic affected you over a long period of time. In this *snapshot* you will need to encapsulate the entire scenario and the dysfunction that took place. Include all people involved, their actions and how you were affected. Describe the beliefs, ideologies or expectations that were placed upon you. Reach for the earliest memory of this dysfunction. If possible, select a point in time where you see and feel yourself as a part of this dynamic to the point of having compassion for yourself within it.

Sample Snapshot for a Long Term Scenario:

My father was "old school"—he worked hard and drank hard too. He worked long hours at his contracting business. He was a good provider, we never lacked for things we wanted or needed, but emotionally he was never available. His role was that of a provider, and that is where all his time and attention went. As a kid, whenever I wanted to do something with him, he would always say: "Maybe later." Later never came for me. I felt unseen and unimportant.

My mother was a staunch churchgoer and was never far from her bible and her rosary. Guilt was the common tool used on both Dad and us kids when she wanted us to do something. When we would question her on it, her reasoning was always: "Because it's God's will!" or: "Because that's what it says in the bible!" She was always punishing us "for our own good," and for things we did or didn't do. We were always doing something bad in the eyes of God. I felt that it didn't matter how "good" I was, I would never be good enough in her eyes or God's.

I took the only escape routes that I knew—the ones I had been shown. I started working hard and drinking hard. At fifteen I started drinking. At sixteen, I dropped out of school and began to work full time.

After completing the *snapshot*, read it out loud to your facilitator, then proceed on to writing your *compassionate letter*.

2) THE COMPASSIONATE LETTER

The *compassionate letter* is a letter written by your current Self to that part of you that went through what you described in your *snapshot* at that time. You now get to take on the role of a friend and/or parent. As a loving friend or parent, you will help this part of you through the scary, unacceptable or dysfunctional thing(s) that happened. You will let your Inner Self know it is not happening anymore, that you are going to keep him/her safe from here on in and that you love and support them unconditionally. Your job now is to create an inner compassionate connection to that life within you, to build a foundation of trust and make him/her feel safe.

It is no secret that as much as 90% of our issues stem from our childhood, so in this letter we refer to our Inner Self as *"Little (Your Name)"* or whatever name you were called at that time. In this letter, acknowledge and validate what **Little (Your Name)** has experienced. Do not hold back, be on his/her side. If you do not validate his/her feelings, then you are not fully on their side. To be completely supportive, you must write this letter with the full belief that what happened to him/her was not right. It was not their fault. And that they did the very best they could at the time.

This is about having compassion for your Self above all else. This is the time to step up and show up for yourself in whatever way is necessary for your Inner Self to feel supported. Even if you perceive yourself as being in the wrong somehow, you will need to take the high road and put your Inner Self's needs first. Also, this is not the time to be concerned with appearing like a victim, now is the time to give *you* what you needed but didn't get. Many find this very difficult to do. This is one of the reasons it is so important to have the help of a facilitator in the beginning.

> *If you do not get in touch with the wounded parts in you, if you do not give them a voice, those screaming, wounded parts of you will continue to run your life.*

On a higher level of awareness, you may know that you go through things for a reason. Whatever happens to you can be said to be of value in defining who and how you are. But the fact is, unless you can validate the fear, anger, shame, etc. of the wounded part of you (really let them know you are on their side), the wounded part of you will not come out of the vicious cycle. He/she will not be able to mature and grow up, which means you cannot move forward.

Sometimes we know too much and go into what I call *spiritual bypass*. This is when your *spiritual knowing* will not let you get angry, blame or express sorrow because you think it is spiritually incorrect, or that you are *above* that. Well, I am here to tell you that if you do not get in touch with the wounded parts in you, if you do not give them a voice and let them be heard—on his/her terms—those screaming, wounded parts of you will continue to run your life.

When that which is within you feels completely safe and has come back into full, natural expression, then and only then will you be able to see that it—the trauma—happened for a reason. To do this, you must first collect back the parts of your inner life that have *split off* and become a whole person again. This means validating what happened to you and allowing all of the feelings that you have surrounding *it* to come out however they need to, and with no judgment, just with love and support. This is called Self-acceptance—a.k.a. Self-love.

HOW TO WRITE YOUR COMPASSIONATE LETTER

Your *compassionate letter* should be handwritten in pen or pencil. It should be a minimum of a half page to a maximum of a full page in length. This too, is to be written in the language you would have used at the time of the *snapshot*. Write until everything that needs to be said is said and is heartfelt and complete. Be as specific as you can. It might start something like this:

Dear Little Joe, I am so sorry for what you went through and for how you were treated. That wasn't right…

THINGS YOU WILL WANT TO TOUCH UPON

- *I am sorry you were treated the way you were, that was not right…*

- *I am so sorry you went through what you did…*

- *I know who you really are, and I know what you have been through and I am so sorry…*

- *You have a right to feel (sad, mad, hurt, etc.)…*

- *It is now safe and okay for you to feel however you feel…*

- *It is not your fault…*

- *You have not done anything wrong…*

- *I am here with you now, you are not alone anymore…*

- *I promise I will never let anything like that happen again (if it is a past trauma experience)…*

- *I promise I will never let you be treated that way again…*

- *You're safe now…*

- *You deserve to be treated with love, kindness and respect…*

- *I love you very much and am here for you now…*

- *Sign your letter with love (Love, Big Joe)*

*This is your chance to show up for yourself. If you do not show up for yourself in this *compassionate letter,* you will not get the full effect of this process.

Men – In general, men tend to have trouble showing compassion for themselves. In our society, males are brought up to be *strong,* and to some that has meant not showing emotion or feeling. Men! Drop that ridiculous mindset. Your life may depend on it. Do not hold back, defend anyone or worry about sounding like a victim. This is for you and your life. Drop your inhibitions around needing to be any certain way and show up for yourself fully now.

Women – In general, women tend to help everyone else at the expense of themselves. Ladies! This is *your* time, take it and use it fully for you. Remember, you cannot give what you do not have. This is your chance to give to yourself, this is your chance to show up for YOU. That being said, you will see a ripple effect go out. You will see you are much more effective and helpful to others when YOU are whole, happy and fulfilled.

3) THE NEXT STEP: CONNECTION AND RELATIONSHIP

Once the *compassionate letter* is completed, the next step is to:

- Re–read the *snapshot* out loud to your facilitator. Go back to that time and actually feel it.

- Go directly into reading your *compassionate letter* out loud to your facilitator. Really mean it. Let the compassion flow. Feel what was going on and give that part what he/she needed at that time.

Immediately after reading these letters, move into the exercise: *Communication with Your Inner Self*, to let your Inner Self respond.

COMMUNICATION WITH YOUR INNER SELF

This is the start of a conversation and communication that does not end with this exercise. You are creating a relationship with your inner life that you will continue to build upon and grow with.

Now is the time to have an open mind. You are now going to let your Inner Self respond. The one responding will be that part of you to whom you just wrote the compassionate letter. **Give this part of you a voice by passing the pen to your *non-dominant* hand, by putting the pen to the page and letting it write**.

Yes, you heard me right, pass the pen to your alternate hand and let your Inner Self respond. Let whatever wants to be written come out. You do not need to *know* anything, and there is nothing for you *to do* except keep an open mind and do your best to just let it happen. It will be as if your alternate hand has a mind of its own and, if you let it write, it will tell you what it thinks and what is going on. The first response will probably not be long, but let your alternate hand write as much as he/she wants. And no, there are no points for neatness!

- Immediately after reading the *compassionate letter*, pass the pen to your non-dominant hand and let your Inner Self respond.

- If you are right-handed, let the left hand write.

- If you are left-handed, let the right hand write.

- Suspend all judgment and expectation.

- No thinking / no analyzing / no editing.

- Just put the pen on the paper and let what wants to be written come out.

- Begin the conversation with your Inner Self (*details below*). Ask questions and offer support with your dominant hand and allow and receive a response to come through the non-dominant hand.

THE ALTERNATE HANDWRITING

The following shows how to effectively follow through with the writing, along with answers to some questions about the writing process.

Remember:

- **Ask the questions and offer support with your dominant hand.**

- **Let your non-dominant hand respond and answer the questions.**

If you were committed and fully involved in the *snapshot* and *compassionate letter* exercises, your emotions are probably close to the surface, and it will be easy to let your Inner Self (that part of you who you wrote to in the *compassionate letter*) respond. People who have a need for control may find it a little harder to let go and let the pen write than those with less need for control. Do not guess or try to know what is coming out, just let what wants to come out to be written. Drop out of your thinking mind. Let your non-dominant hand take over. You will discover that your alternate hand knows what it wants to write.

Through doing this alternate handwriting exercise you may discover that, at the beginning, your Inner Self is shy or afraid, but he/she really does want to be listened to and heard. They would not have shown themselves otherwise. You will also see that they have very valuable information that is pertinent and directly related to the negative pattern going on in your life right now. This inner life holds the keys to your healing. When you make a good connection, you will understand this right away, because you will feel it and know.

When offering reassurance with the dominant hand, end every sentence with a question. This will prompt the Inner Self to respond. Basic prompts may go something like this: "Okay? … All right? … Do you understand? … Would you like that?"

This is a sample of the writing that may take place starting with the alternate hand's response to the compassionate letter.

The Alternate hand (AH), the Dominant Hand (DH)

AH: *Thank you for being here with me.*

DH: *Of course, I know what you have been through, Little _____. I am sorry that happened. Are you okay?*

AH: *I'm scared.*

DH: *I am sorry you are scared. Thank you for telling me how you feel. Why are you afraid?*

AH: *I'm all alone.*

DH: *I'm here with you now, to love and look after you. You're not alone anymore. Do you understand that?*

AH: *I guess…*

DH: *You are safe now Little _____. Do you know that?*

AH: *I think so.*

DH: *What can I do to help you to feel safe?*

AH: *Just you being here talking with me feels nice.*

DH: *Okay, I can do that. I am here for you now, and I promise I will not go away and leave you alone anymore, all right?*

AH: *That would be nice.*

DH: *Do you trust me?*

AH: *(No answer.)*

DH: *It's okay if you don't or if you don't know. I am here and promise to love and look after you no matter what, okay?*

AH: *I like that.*

Here is what it may look like. Let your alternate hand write whatever it wants to write. Do not worry about neatness. Let this part of you speak (write) as much or as little as they want to.

Thank you for being here with me

Of course Little Jessie. I know what you have been going through, and I am so sorry that you were treated that way. are you okay?

I am scared

I'm sorry you're scared, it's okay for you to feel however you feel though. Why are you scared?

I'm all al one

I'm here with you now to protect and look after you. You are not alone anymore. Do you understand that?

Okay

I'm here with you, and you are safe now Little Jessie. Alright?

I guess so

What do you need to feel safe?

You being here with me feels good.

okay. great. I'm here with you and I promise I'm not going anywhere, okay?

I would like that

Do you trust me Little Jessie?

(No response)

It's okay if you don't, or if you don't know. I promise that I am here with you now, and that I will not leave you alone any more, okay?

Thank you

ASKING QUESTIONS

– Whether you are aware of it or not, this Inner Self has been the prime drive behind your life up until now. Get to know this Inner Self, it is in your best interest. The phrase "know thyself" will take on a new level of meaning now, and will start to make much more sense as you do this process.

First and foremost, understand the importance of reassuring this Inner Self that you are there for them and are on their side. Be sure to ask questions that will make him/her feel safe and cared about. Ask simple questions that will draw them out and give them room to speak. You want them to speak so you can get to know them. Ask how they are doing, what they need, what they are thinking, what they like and what they do not like.

Your Inner Self may not be used to being asked: "How are you?" He/she may not be used to having someone show an interest or care about them at all. Remind them that you are there for them, you love them, you are on their side and they can trust you.

Find out what they want or need. Realize that this part of you has literally been locked away and unheard for a very long time. Do not be in a rush for them to trust you, just get to know them by asking simple questions. Be on a loving mission to understand and learn about this life within you.

You will most likely have some emotions come up in the beginning. Be kind and gentle with yourself. This is the start of parenting this wounded part of you out of trauma and learning how to give them what they need to feel safe. Remember, it is of utmost importance that this be done gently and with understanding and compassion. You are building trust here. Understand you are likely talking to a child. **How would you talk to a *child* that had been hurt or abused?** I would hope you would be full of care, kindness and have patience with them. This is what is required.

LOWERING RESISTANCE

– There is always some level of resistance in the beginning. Our conditioned thinking mind (primarily controlled by the left brain) dislikes what it does not understand. It is driven to *know* and cannot stand being out of control. *NTHP* is abstract and our ego feels threatened by it. Often it will hold onto a sense of control by doing what it can to prevent you from going forward. Be aware of thought patterns that put blocks up for you such as: "This makes no sense! … I have too much to do right now … This is ridiculous … I can't do this … This is too much for me … This doesn't work on me … I'm too damaged."

> **It is important to pass the pen over to your alternate hand *right away*, without thinking, and to just let it write.** Do not give your left brain (your logical, controlling mind) enough time to get in there and start to question it. The left brain will try to take control and prevent you from allowing your subconscious to speak.

Realize that resistance is normal in the beginning. We *think!* That is just the way it is in this game of being human. Know your thoughts are secondary in this exercise, and they are not to dominate it. Pay no attention to them and allow what wants to be written by your alternate hand to come out.

As best you can, be in a place of non-resistance and drop the control of your thinking mind. Continue to ask questions and offer support with your dominant hand, passing the pen to your alternate hand right away for the response. The resistance will become less and less as you keep going, and your answers will become purer and clearer. This is the building of a relationship, and it takes time and effort. You will see that being compassionately persistent with yourself will pay off. Over time, you will see that your alternate handwriting will come purely from your subconscious, and you will know it.

IF THEY ARE SCARED
– If in their response to you they say they are scared, let them know: "I am sorry you are scared, *and it is okay for you to feel that way.*" Ask what it is that is scaring them. Align with them by saying things like:

- *I am on your side...*

- *It is safe for you to feel however you feel now...*

- *You are not alone anymore…*

- *I care about you…*

- *I am here to love and protect you from now on…*

IF THEY ARE ANGRY

– Once again, let them know: "I am sorry you are angry, but it is okay that you feel that way. Why are you angry?" Acknowledge and show compassion for the situation they are experiencing. Ask them what they need, and how they would like you to help. Assure them you want to help. Align with them by saying things like:

- *You have every right to feel angry...*

- *You do not need to go through this alone anymore…*

- *I am on your side and want to help you…*

- *Nothing you say will change how I feel about you. You are safe to tell me how you feel...*

IF THEY ARE ANGRY WITH YOU!

It happens occasionally that the Inner Self/child will be angry with you in the beginning. It is a time when you need to stay on the high road and let this wounded part of you know it is okay for him/her to feel however they feel. Give them this freedom by telling them: "I am sorry you are angry with me, but it is okay that you feel that way. Why are you angry with me?" This reassures them that it is safe for them to express it to you and you will not get angry with them or shut them out. It lets them know you are on their side and that you are a safe person for them. This is key in *unfreezing* from the trauma that has been holding them hostage. This is a time when it is imperative that you have a facilitator who understands this work and what is needed, given that it can be very confronting for someone to hear: "I hate you!" coming from inside of them. Understand that underneath this anger is hurt, and that this inner part of ourselves needs to go through the anger to allow itself to get to the hurt that leads to the undercurrent of love.

Be patient with this type of scenario. It takes loving persistence and compassion to lead him/her out of anger, but it will happen. This shows you how you have been treating yourself, and it is your opportunity to change the pattern.

IF THEY DON'T TRUST YOU

– In this conversation between your dominant hand and your alternate hand, you are opening up and talking to parts of you that have been closed away and ignored for potentially a very long time. You can understand why your Inner Self may not trust you. Do not take this personally, you did not know!

If he/she is wary or mistrustful of you, say to them:

Dominant Hand: *I'm sorry that you don't trust me, but it's okay that you don't. Why don't you trust me?*

Alternate Hand: *Because you left me and have ignored me.*

DH: *I'm sorry that I ignored you, I didn't know. I do know now, though, and I promise I won't ignore you anymore. Okay?*

This is what they need to hear, a voice that is gentle and caring that wants to help them. For some people, showing up for themselves in this way can be very difficult.

IF THEY ARE SAD

– Once again, let them know, "I am sorry you are sad, but it is okay that you feel that way. It is safe for you to feel however you feel. Why are you sad?" Align with them by saying things like:

- *I am sorry you were treated that way. That was not right…*

- *I am here to love, look after and protect you from now on…*

- *You are my first priority…*

- *You do not have to go through this alone anymore...*

- *I promise to treat you with the love and respect you deserve...*

IF THEY ARE HAPPY

– Even if the response comes out positive and happy and nothing appears wrong for them, aligning with them is still important. They have shown themselves to you for a reason. They may have something important to share with you or perhaps being *happy* is an automated, learned response to being asked how they are. Regardless of the reason they have shown themselves to you, it is your job to find out what they want or need. Align with them by asking: "I am glad you are happy, that makes me feel good. Is there a reason why you are feeling so good?"

IF THERE IS NO RESPONSE

– If nothing comes out of your alternate hand in the beginning, do not force anything. This work is gentle and easy. If nothing comes out, then pose this question with your dominant hand: "Are you okay?" and then pass the pen over for them to answer again. Be sure to give some space here. Do not rush it. Put the pen in the alternate hand. Put the pen on the page and let go.

If still nothing comes from the alternate hand, then you can pose the same question with your dominant hand: "Are you all right?" Only this time, on the line below, write the word "yes" on one side of the page and "no" further across on the same line. Make sure there is space between both words. Pass the pen over to your non-dominant hand and let it circle one or the other. Your hand will be drawn to the word that holds a charge. Let your hand circle whichever one it wants to.

If this is the way your writing starts, you will know there is a level of fear involved. Your Inner Self is resistant to trusting you, and you will need to patiently build that trust and safety for him/her. Be gentle and take time to make this part of you feel safe enough to come out and talk. Offer support with your dominant hand and keep asking yes/no questions until the writing emerges from the alternate hand.

IF THEY ARE IN DANGER, PANIC, PAIN OR FEEL OVERWHELMED (*RETRIEVING SOMEONE FROM A TRAUMA MEDITATION)

– This guided meditation is to be used when through the alternate handwriting you encounter an inner child or adult in distress, panic or pain. It is also to be used if an inner child or adult asks for help or a hug.

This guided meditation is an important step in stopping an ongoing trauma that continues to trigger and haunt you. What you are going to do in this exercise is go to the subconscious level and literally take the Inner Self out of the experience of the trauma, where it is still going on. When you consciously do that, the trauma simply stops, it just ceases to operate. The wounded part of you will experience leaving the scenario—when it was happening, and will therefore accept and know that *it is not happening anymore.*

*Understand that you are not forcing this Inner Self to come with you. This retrieval is only done after building a significant level of trust and receiving the consent and desire of the Inner Self to do so. It is to be done in an easy and harmonious manner.

> *One needs a willingness to be exposed to the unconscious.*
> *This requires some courage and persistence. We can't call up*
> *the unconscious at will. … Normally, emotions need to be*
> *expressed in some way in order to be processed. Emotions*
> *are energy. If they are not processed, they become blocks in*
> *our bodies and nervous systems to the free flow of our energy*
> *systems and of grace.*
>
> ~ *Thomas Keating*

For this realization to truly sink in, the Inner Self may still need to be reminded a few times through the alternate writing that they are safe, loved, loveable and protected. But after this retrieval, they will likely come back to remembering quickly.

For more information and the full **Retrieval From a Past Trauma** guided meditation, please refer to the **Guided Meditations / Exercises** chapter of this book.

The audio versions of the guided meditations can be downloaded from this site:

www.reclaimyourpowerprocess.com

BUILDING A HEALTHY RELATIONSHIP

ARE YOU ACTING LIKE YOUR PARENTS?!

It is worth noting here that people tend to treat themselves the same way their parents treated them. This is fine if your parents treated you well. But for those whose parents didn't, it is important to understand that it is likely because you were brought up by parents who were themselves wounded as children. If this was the case, outrageous as it seems, our models for being a grown-up and a parent are these wounded children. Whether we are aware of it or not, our parents/caregivers became gods in our eyes, and we took in everything they taught us. The tendency that came from this is to do things just like our parents did or, if it was too painful, exactly the opposite.

With this information, be aware of how you are treating your Inner Self. For most of you this will be the very first time this Inner Self has been given a voice and is being listened to and heard. Let him/her know they are safe and loved—that's it. No judgment, criticism or making them feel bad or wrong. You may have the desire to try and fix them, make them better or maybe even treat them the same way you were treated growing up. Just be aware that you want to do things differently this time. Parent this Inner Self with utmost gentleness, compassion and understanding.

DO NOT GIVE ADVICE!

Do not give your Inner Self advice or tell him/her that they are fine. Find out *from them* how they are, what is going on for them, and what they need. Let them know that they are not alone anymore, that you are fully on their side, that they are safe and that you are looking after them from now on.

That is it. No discipline or advice or trying to *break through it*. That will blow it for you and destroy the trust you are building, trust that is necessary for this wounded part of you to *unfreeze*. You are there to serve them. You are on their clock, going at the pace they need.

It is this connection that is the healing. Be a good friend to your Inner Self and watch the healing naturally occur.

GIVE THEM WHAT THEY WANT OR NEED

– The first level of trust is established by consistently showing up for your Inner Self through this writing; the second level of trust is created by **asking them what they want or need and giving it to them.** Every time you connect with them through the alternate writing you are, at some point, going to ask them: "How can I help you? Is there something you want or need?" The point of this writing is to understand what will make these wounded parts of you feel safe and able to develop in a natural, healthy way. This means taking on the role of a good, loving parent by giving them what they need to heal.

A couple of things happen when you do this. The first is he/she will come to understand that it is now safe and good to ask for what they want and need. If you were never asked what you wanted or needed growing up, or if you were shut down or punished for trying to have your needs met, your Inner Self may find it very difficult to tell you what they need. You must continually remind him or her that it is now safe and good for them to ask for what they need until they can fully grasp and accept that idea.

The second thing that happens when this inner life gets their wants and needs met by you is: they will gain the belief system that they can ask for what they want—and they will get it! Not a bad belief system to have working within you. Don't worry, they do not want diamonds and yachts and trips around the world. They want you. Your inner child may want to do things like: go to the playground, talk with you more, have a bubble bath, go to a movie, play with a doll, read a certain type of book or story, have a nap, go to the beach, etc. Yes, when dealing with an inner child there is going to be some childhood things that you will need to fulfill. Do not worry, though, you will not have to play with dolls or sit in a sandbox for two years. This work tends to travel quite quickly. You can almost consider it symbolic that the simple act of showing up consistently to do these specific tasks automatically creates a bond of trust that will pay off as a solid foundation of trust in your life.

You will discover a wonderful thing at this time. Whatever it is your little self asks for feels really good to do! It will seem very strange, but as you color the model or ride the bike or swing on the swings, it will start to feel warm and really good inside you! This is the power of the child, the magic inside you, and this will be where you get to fully experience how alive, how beautiful and how expressive this life within you is.

You will begin to see how powerful this aspect of your being is as the things that it requests just show up for you, as if by magic. You will begin to experience the power of this inner life.

The child is in me still and sometimes not so still.

~ Fred Rogers

DO WHAT YOU SAY YOU ARE GOING TO DO!

Follow through with what you say you will do. If you do not, your Inner Self will be hurt or disappointed, if not angry. If your inner child becomes upset with you, you will see this disappointment (hurt) manifest in your present-day occurrences. Things may suddenly not work out or become more difficult, and you will experience more turmoil and dysfunction in your life. It will seem as if there is something working against you—because there is. This is a great lesson that shows us the power of what is going on within us, and what happens to us when we do not follow through for ourselves. When we do not do what we say we are going to do, we lose the trust of our Inner Self. This may make them withdraw even further. Other people not believing in you is one thing, but when you do not believe within yourself, that is a deeper level of mistrust that will cause a downward spiral.

CONSISTENCY IS KEY

– The main pillar of this work is safety. Without the feeling of safety, nothing changes, and it will feel like pulling teeth to get your Inner Self to open up and cooperate with you.

When I first started this work and felt this amazing connection to the life within me, I wrote pretty much every day for three years. Like any healthy relationship, it takes time and effort. This one is no different. The foundation of love is trust. Trust is created through consistency, and that consistency is fashioned by continually showing up for our Self and doing the alternate handwriting (daily, at the beginning). This is where the connection is made and the trust is established. Your Inner Self will then begin to *unfreeze*, warm up and develop into the powerfully loving person he/she is, that you are—naturally and easily. This is the foundation that the relationship stands firmly on.

> The foundation of love is trust. Trust is created through consistency. The consistency comes from us continually showing up for ourselves through the alternate handwriting.

Understand that you will not be dealing with wounded parts of you forever, or even for very long, for that matter. Yes, you must do the healing work first, but the connection will turn to warm, loving and wise guidance. As Dr. Bradshaw says, "The wounded child becomes the wonder child."

The wounded child becomes the wonder child.

~ Dr. John Bradshaw

DAILY WRITING - CONSISTENTLY CONNECT WITH YOUR INNER SELF

– Your daily writing is going to start like this:

"Hi, how are you, and how old are you right now?"

You do not have to do a *snapshot* every time you write to your Inner Self. Start the conversation by asking them how they are doing and how old they are.

In the beginning, connect with your Inner Self every day. It does not have to be for a long period, but if you can consistently connect in the morning for at least ten to twenty minutes before you go about your day, that alone will yield incredible benefits for you.

There will be times when your Inner Self wants to talk with you for longer, though, so be sure and give yourself the time to allow this inner life to be fully heard and felt. If you are writing and they want to talk for longer than you are able to accommodate, or they ask you to do something you cannot get to for some time, just ask them: "Would it be alright if we continue this conversation once I get home from work?" or "We can't do that right now, would it be all right if we did it on Saturday?" Likely it will be fine with them; however, **you must remember to follow through on your promises.**

If you encounter an upset, always ask what they need and how you can help them. Do not ignore them and leave them to deal with it on their own. If you do, you will feel the energy of that part of you until you address it. Find out what they need and give it to them. You will not necessarily have to give them something. It is more about being there for them, connecting with them and making them feel recognized, safe and loved.

These conversations will become more and more connected, enjoyable, and eventually, inspiring and enlightening. Take it one patient and loving step at a time, though. Let them guide you by their clock. In this process, their clock is the master clock.

The reason you ask them their age is because it is important to know the age of whom you are talking to and the time they are in. Whoever needs your attention will come up, so asking their age will point you to what is going on for them. It will most likely be something you recall. If not, ask them more questions to find out what is happening for them.

There are certain basic developmental needs at various stages, and it is good to know what they are. (You can see the *Developmental Ages and Stages* in Part 3.) Knowing the stages can give you some understanding ahead of time of what his/her needs may be. *Do not go into the writing with any preconceived ideas about what they need, or what you are going to do, though. Get all of the information and guidance about how they are and what they say they need from them.* This is the process at work. Let it guide you, not the other way around.

Continue to align with them through the alternate handwriting as described above until it feels complete. Make sure you have asked what they want or need and have either fulfilled it or set a time to fulfill it.

ALWAYS SIGN OFF STRONG

– At the end of every writing session you want to leave your Inner Self feeling safe, loved and at peace. This may feel like a big thing to accomplish in the beginning if you are dealing with some strong wounding. Your Inner Self may not fully believe you in the beginning, but as you continually tell them that:

- They are safe

- You love them

- You completely accept them just as they are

- You are there for them whenever they need you

- You are glad they are here

- You are very proud of them

- They are number one in your life

- You know who they really are

- You thank them for being there with you and talking to you

- You will always love and be there for them no matter what

...it will eventually sink in that they are safe, loved and cared about. You obviously would not say all of these things every time you sign off with them. You will find during the writing what needs to be said in the sign off. Reassurances should be directly related to that writing.

An example of a sign off:

Thank you so much for being here and speaking with me. Know that I'm here for you whenever you want or need me. I'm very proud of you. I love you and appreciate you very much. I look forward to speaking with you again very soon.

Love, Big You

IT IS NOT HAPPENING ANYMORE

– The parts of you that are going to come up in this process are ones that have been wounded, the ones that have disconnected from your current Self. They are most likely going to be experiencing the negative event in real time. We have called upon the part of you that is the cause of the dysfunction you are experiencing in your life right now through the *snapshot*. He/she is the part of you that is still stuck back in that time, and to this part of you that trauma is still going on and is very much alive and real.

As this part of you starts to understand and trust what you are telling them, they will calm down and you will feel it! In this present moment You will calm down, slow down, see more clearly, feel lighter and happier, all because they are alive inside of you.

A significant aspect of helping this part to *unfreeze* is to let them know that: "It is not happening anymore." If they are still stuck in that experience and continually re-experiencing it, simply telling them it isn't, will not be true for them. Telling them that what they have been going through for so many years "is not happening anymore," could bring up some real emotion, because that experience is all that this part of you has known until now. He/she could get the idea right away and start to *unfreeze*, or they may become resistant and call you "mean" or a "liar" for saying that the hell they are experiencing is not actually happening. You will want to make a good connection with them and have them trust you before you say this to them, but any part of you still going through trauma needs to be told that: "It is not happening any longer." They will get it eventually, some quickly, some more slowly. Understand that it is like pulling a person out of another world and telling them that their world is not real anymore. That is exactly what you are doing, so have compassion, understanding and empathy for them while they come to terms with this.

What comes with this realization is the knowledge that they are safe now, and until they know they can trust you, they will not feel the safety needed to let go of that old experience. You are there to gently bring them into the present moment again, where the threat does not exist, and peace naturally prevails. This is where this work is both profound and magical. As this part of you starts to understand and trust what you are telling them, they will calm down and you will feel it! In this present moment *You* will calm down, slow down, see more clearly, feel lighter and happier, all because they are alive inside of you.

THE GATEKEEPER

– During the process of alternate writing you may encounter a *gatekeeper*. The *gatekeeper* often comes up for people who are predominantly left-brained and have a strong need for control. It tends to arise more commonly in males than in females, but regardless of gender its presence is due to a deep-seated fear and mistrust that tends to stem from some form of past trauma. The *gatekeeper* is our programmed thinking mind's need to retain control of the situation. It is more comfortable with the pain it knows than the uncertainty of what change might bring. It is usually quite obvious when the *gatekeeper* jumps in, because it brings into the writing current time and current circumstances. As an example, if you made a connection to your seven-year-old Self and then your alternate hand referred to something happening in your life yesterday, something that seven-year-old Self could not have experienced or even known about, then this is the *gatekeeper* stepping in. This tends to occur when you are getting close to something that is significant and has strong energy around it.

The writing might go something like this:

Dominant Hand: *I'm sorry he treated you that way, that wasn't right. How can I help you, what do you need?*

Alternate Hand: *I need you to go and tell our boss that we're not working this long weekend and that we want more money.*

In this example, the non-dominant hand (the seven-year-old) would not know your boss. Seven-year-old children do not work or have bosses, they do not care about time off or more money. All of that is coming from the present time. As silly as this example may seem, it is a common occurrence for a person struggling to keep life predictable.

Realize that there is no healing from this place. Trying to change things from your current conscious mind will have you chasing your tail. Ultimately, this type of writing is you talking to yourself at the conscious level. It is true that you will be able to create some great vocabulary and affirmations, but you are not dealing with the looping belief or experience that is occurring in the subconscious mind. No real change or healing can come from this type of conscious dialogue.

If you find yourself with a *gatekeeper*, first, simply ask them if it would be okay if you talked to Little _____ at age seven again. It may be as simple as that. But if your *gatekeeper* is keeping you from connecting to the younger parts of you, you can express your concern for the little one and ask the *gatekeeper* if they understand that it is now safe and good to feel and go back there, that it is in the name of a better life. Let that conversation happen until they agree to let you talk with the little one. Sometimes the *gatekeeper* can be very stubborn, playing games with you or just being adamant about preventing you from connecting with the little one. When this

> *You cannot get from the outer world what you cannot give to yourself. When you give yourself what you want and need within you, then it will show up on the outside—it has to. Your outer world is simply a mirror showing you what is going on inside of you.*

type of *gatekeeper* appears, what I have learned to do as a facilitator is to simply hand the writing back to the client by asking them: "What would you like to say to the *gatekeeper*?" and let the client speak directly to the *gatekeeper* through the writing. This will show the facilitator where the client is at—their desire and their level of willingness and desire to proceed.

This also reveals to the client the fear that this part of them has about moving toward change. This awareness can be a powerful realization. There is nothing the facilitator can do with an unwilling client. As harsh as this may seem, it hands the ball back to them, and if the client really wants the healing, then eventually the *gatekeeper* will stop jumping in.

Having said all of this, it is important to honor the *gatekeeper* as a part of your inner life and not make him/her feel bad or wrong. You created them out of necessity. They have been there, on guard to protect and keep you safe. I remember when I first connected with the part of me that was protecting my heart. I saw myself standing in freezing cold weather wearing only a light sweater with the sleeves rolled up. I was solid, stoic and completely unemotional. When I made an emotional connection to him, to my total surprise I burst into tears. For all of my adult life and most of my childhood, this part had been standing on guard for me, preventing anything from coming near my heart that could hurt me.

My *gatekeeper* was doing his job, guarding me. Without him, I may not have survived the way I did. You need to let that part of you know that it is now safe, that they can relax and have a rest. Assure them that it is safe to go inside and connect with Little _____ now, and that you will be gentle, and that they can trust you.

LEARNING HOW TO NAVIGATE ... AGAIN

Now that you have a better understanding of trauma and have opened the door to your subconscious, you can apply the healing principals of this process. I am sure some of your heads are swimming right now. The logical mind does not naturally comprehend this type of abstract work and does not know what to do with it. This initial *untangling* process of "who is the wounded child and who am I, and where do we separate?" takes time. You will encounter many signposts and insights along the way as you reclaim these parts of your Self. It turns into a magnificent ride as fragmented parts of you return warmly back into your Self, taking you from feeling broken to feeling whole.

When your relationship with your Inner Self is in place and healthy, all other relationships in your life will transform for the better. If your relationship with your Self is not based in complete safety, trust and love, neither will be the other ones in your life. Life is an inside job. What is going on inside of you at the level of your subconscious mind creates what you experience in your outer world.

Continue to write and connect to the life within you daily. Watch the profound effect it has on how you feel and how your interactions with people in your life gently and wonderfully transform. You cannot get from the outer world what you cannot give to yourself. When you give yourself what you want and need within you, then it will show up on the outside—it has to. Your outer world is simply a mirror showing you what is going on inside of you.

You have found the keys, and now it is time to learn how to drive the vehicle. Don't worry, the process will show you how. Go on to the *Evolution and Development* section to continue on with your work of learning how to navigate the subconscious mind.

Client Testimonial:

*The **NTHP** has completely freed me from my past … I have been dealing with a childhood sexual abuse issue for the better part of my adult life, I have done a lot of counseling for it, but never got anywhere with it. I would just shut down and it wasn't effective for me.*

*I've never experienced anything like this [**NTHP**] before. This work took me to a place I've never been in my life, and honestly didn't think I would be able to get to … Today I have a really big smile on my face because I don't live in the past anymore. I really didn't realize I could have this kind of freedom … I'm not stuck and frozen anymore. I'm finally able to start progressing in my life again! It feels like a fog has been lifted … I'm excited about my life now!*

Part 3

THE EVOLUTION AND DEVELOPMENT

Now that a connection has been made with your Inner Self, and now that you are in the process of developing a healthy relationship with it, the next step is to understand the natural stages that will occur. The *Evolution and Development* section speaks about what happens as a result of doing the alternate handwriting and addresses how this relationship changes and grows. While this change and growth is a simple and natural progression, it is essential for the facilitator to understand the evolution of development that occurs through the work. When healed, the subconscious is the gateway to higher consciousness.

UNTANGLING

We human beings can become deeply entangled with our emotions, so much so that they can completely overtake us. We think that the emotion we are experiencing is who we are in that moment. *Untangling* is the ability to separate from the emotion of our past negative experiences, and see our current moment with a new clarity. Being *untangled* is to be fully present in the current moment and experiencing it as it really is *now*, without any influences or triggers that stem from the past. When we are able to get enough distance from the emotion (a mental or neurological distancing created through the *NTHP* process) we are able to feel the energy without it taking us over. This is how we reclaim our power of choice, and until we have the power of choice over our emotions, we are at the mercy of them.

Without *untangling*, we are merely coping. We may create a forced sense of control by suppressing our reactions when we are triggered, but doing this will either turn into withdrawal or depression or become a ticking bomb that will eventually go off.

People who struggle to control their emotions are often directed to use a behavioral medication. As I stated earlier in the book, there is a time and place for behavioral medication, but for many this is an unnecessary prescription. Medications mask what is really going on inside and cover over the part of us that has come up for healing. The medications that mask our emotions have the ability to keep us from finding the lasting healing we desire.

In order to *untangle* ourselves from our past, we need to be able to be present with it. This is where the gift of the alternate writing comes in. When emotions come up in us, we know that it is something in us that has come up for healing. When we have this awareness, we can take a healthy approach to our emotions and how we feel. We will remember that our emotions are not who we are but are instead the wounded or traumatized part of us that needs and wants our love and attention. We can give this love and attention easily and generously through the alternate writing. This awareness is the first step to Self-acceptance and Self-love, and it comes from having compassion for our feelings, however they are.

> *When emotion comes up in us, it is a part within us that has come up for healing.*

Through the process we will *untangle* our Self from our emotions and be able to *be* with them and not react to them. The alternate writing will allow us to connect with the parts of us that are feeling these emotions and help us to understand why these parts of us are feeling the way they are. We will be able to love, console, support and let them know that whatever they are experiencing is not happening any longer.

You will know you have *untangled* when you ask the question in your writing: "Hi, how are you, and how old are you right now?" and the answer comes back with a positive and healthy response from your alternate hand consistently, over a significant period of time (ten days–two weeks). When this happens, you are ready to move into the empowerment aspect of your work.

GAINING TRACTION

We gain *Traction* on our Self when we complete the inner work that is required to create a consistently harmonious relationship with the life within us. Having *traction* is possibly the most significant stage of healing.

Once we have done this inner work, nothing more is needed to sustain it. Peace is within us easily and naturally, because it is our foundational nature. At this point, we realize that to be who we truly are is effortless. There is no technique to do, no pill to take, nor any ritual that needs to be performed in order to sustain it. We can stop seeking outside of our Self. Very few people in this day and age have inner peace and harmony. It is a difficult concept for some people to accept, that life does not have to be hard or a struggle, that life can be a peaceful and harmonious experience. Anyone who has come this far in the *NTHP* understands that their peace comes from the inner connection to their Self and from listening to and giving their inner life what it wants and needs.

The game changes at this level of our spiritual development. Until now, we have been giving our Inner Self what he/she has needed to grow up and develop, but as we move forward the *giving* turns into *following*. With *traction* on our Self, we get to follow the guidance that comes from our now-healthy and whole inner life. As we learn the power of this inner life, very quickly we realize that it is in our best interest to follow the guidance that it offers us. We will understand it will not steer us wrong, and that our intuition becomes acutely accurate and that we can trust it. True power and success comes from the life within us, not from the people or things outside of us.

As I have stated the *NTHP* is not a quick fix, it is a relationship. This relationship is the foundation of all of our relationships, one we will grow with as this inner life grows. Healing does not occur with the flick of a switch. As the inner parts of us develop in a healthy way, we will see that so, too, does the wisdom and guidance that comes from it. We will have access to a wisdom far greater than what we are currently aware of or could humanly know.

In my next book, *Unleash Your Genius*, we will introduce you to the next step, the *Soul Re-Cognition Process*. **Soul Re-Cognition (SRC)** has its foundation in the *NTHP* but travels beyond into the next natural phase of empowerment. With *SRC* you will connect with different aspects of your being and be guided in bringing yourself into full Self-expression—naturally.

SELF-LOVE

Self-love is a confusing and misunderstood term. What does it mean? How do you do it? Do I stand in front of the mirror and tell myself how great and lovely I am? Honestly, that is not a bad idea, but affirmations and good intentions will only take us so far. In the alternate writing work, we receive clarity on exactly how *we* uniquely need to be loved. We will be shown what we needed growing up but did not get. We will come to know what we need to do now to make up for it and to bridge the gap by offering the safety, confidence, attention, nurturing, compassion, acceptance or whatever was needed at the time. This is Self-love. Purely and simply it means having a healthy, loving and harmonious relationship with the life inside of you—respecting and honoring the different aspects within you.

NTHP will prove to us, in no uncertain terms, how powerful we are, and it all stems from understanding and learning how to love our Self.

As we continue on with the practice of honoring, listening to and fulfilling the requests of our Inner Self, life flows more smoothly with synchronicity and our outer relationships miraculously become more kind and loving to match.

Is it miraculous or is it by design? Is it magic or is it our nature? *The outer world simply mirrors back to us how we are treating our Self.* That is the big secret. You may be asking, "Where does he get off making such a radical declaration?!" I can say it because this work has blatantly shown it to me.

If we want to know how we are treating our (inner) Self, we need only to look out into our world and see what is coming back to us. If we do not like what we see and want to improve our life, then we must go inside. Go inside and find out where we are treating our Self in a way that is discordant or out of harmony with our true nature. **By going inside, we are guided in how to care for, respect and give to our Self the way *we* need. This is how we learn to love ourselves.**

The deeper reality of this is yes, we can change our world, by changing how we treat our Self. *NTHP* will prove to us, under no uncertain terms, how powerful we are, and it all stems from understanding and learning how to love our Self.

FORGIVENESS

Forgiveness is another term that needs to be re-examined in today's society. So often we are told to: "Just drop the past and move on. Forget about it, it is over and done with." If only it were that simple. As you are learning here and probably have been well aware from life experience, any highly emotional negative experience not dealt with at the time of the event, will be held within the walls of the body until it is brought into conscious awareness and dealt with in a healthy way. The perception that we can simply make the decision to forgive someone who has harmed, hurt or wronged us is misguided. It is not possible to feel the release of true forgiveness from a cerebral place alone.

Forgiving simply from our conscious mind is conceptual and can even be harmful. Whether consciously or unconsciously keeping that energy down, not letting it come up by denying it or trying to hide it, is an emotional time bomb. Without a doubt, the emotion inside will come out eventually. If it comes out of its own accord it will be a pressured and uncontrollable reaction that can destroy relationships, careers, finances, etc. If it is held back long enough and not diffused, it will come out as disease in the body.

It is true, we must consciously make the decision to forgive, but just saying and wanting it to be so is not enough. If we claim: "I have forgiven," but still have an injured or angry feeling bubbling inside us, or the negative pattern continues to happen, then we are not experiencing true forgiveness. We cannot forgive if we still have wounded energy operating in us. To forgive does not mean what happened to us is now okay or that the perpetrator is now somehow absolved of his/her wrongdoing. In fact, forgiveness is less about the person who has wronged us and more about giving the negative energy we carry within us back to the time it originally happened.

So how do we get to the point of forgiving and having peace within? There is a hint in the word itself: *for-give*—give back. We give the negative energy back to the time of the event; again, it is now less about the perpetrator than about our entanglement with the experience.

To forgive is an experience of the body where tension, tightness and negative emotion are released. Once we are free of that energy, we are no longer in its grip—we have forgiven, given the energy back and, in the process, liberated our Self. The story of what happened has not changed, only now we are no longer living it. We can look at what happened to us, our experience, and not be afraid of it or react to it, because it is no longer a part of us and we can move forward from it. This experience shows us the complete interconnectedness of the body and the mind.

Until we reach the energetic place within us where the negative experience is held within our body, that painful energy will continue to cycle. When we give it back to that time, it will dissipate and we will return to our natural Self. From this place there is nothing more to let go of. We will feel it in our physical body and we will *just know* it has happened. As the saying goes: "The issue is in the tissue."

To truly forgive, it is essential to reach the place that holds the painful energy and allow it to come forth again. Only then can the painful energy be released and given back to that time. This may mean going through the original fear, anger, sorrow, grief or sadness again. However, the difference this time is that we have the ability to support our Self through these difficult emotions and phases by using the alternate writing. Through the writing and connecting process, the pain of the issue will arise, and we can bring the wounded part of us into the present moment where *it is not happening anymore, and we are safe.*

As we give to our Self what we need to release the energy and *give it back* to that time, we come out of being disconnected from our present Self to feeling whole, at peace and in love for one's Self. This coming home often has a wonderful side effect. It can lead to a greater understanding and compassion, not just for our Self but also for the others who were involved, and a higher vision of the event itself.

BOUNDARIES

When I facilitate people through this process, I am always amazed how positive changes occur naturally for them without any strenuous effort. Understand that when we facilitate this process we do not coach. I was a coach for over fifteen years prior to the development of this work, and I no longer coach; I no longer have to. People get their information and guidance from within themselves, not from the facilitator or anyone else. How could I possibly know your wants and needs better than you? Between sessions, a facilitator of NTHP may give people exercises or tasks to aid their healing, but these tasks come from the direct guidance of the Inner Self through the alternate handwriting of the client. It is also unnecessary for an NTHP facilitator to coach someone into setting boundaries or standing up for themselves. Working from the outside in is trying to change the effect, and is, in fact, working backwards. As we have discovered, when the inside changes, the outside naturally and easily follows suit.

Boundaries are, of course, very important, but often people are afraid to take action and implement them for themselves and others. In this work I see people naturally and calmly setting boundaries for themselves without any animosity or hesitation. It is amazing to watch someone who was too timid or scared to set boundaries become confident and sure of themselves. Many times, it surprises and delights both them and me.

Boundaries are indicators of how we are honoring and standing up for our Self. If we do not honor our Self, then no one else will either; if we do not respect our Self, then neither will anyone else. When we start to show our Self the love, respect and honor we deserve, the outer experience and many times our outer actions, quite simply change as well. We come to the very obvious realization that we deserve to be treated with kindness. If people have not been treating us that way, they either naturally stop acting that way or they leave our life.

As Napoleon Hill so simply put it: "We are senders and receivers of messages." What we send out is what we will get back, and what we get back is what we have been giving our Self. When our low vibrations of *not good enough, can't* and *don't deserve* shift to the higher vibrations of *I am a good person, I deserve to be treated with love and respect* and *I can do what I want to do*, then the outer world and our actions simply change. No, we do not put ourselves at risk, but we do wake up to the fact that we have not been supporting our Self and we deserve better.

You don't get what you want, you get what you are.

~ Wayne Dyer

ANGER

As I have told many clients: "If you don't pursue it, it will pursue you." I am speaking of what is going on inside of us. What is going on inside of us will eventually come out, but if we do not pursue and go to it, then it will come out in ways that are uncontrolled and can destroy relationships, our career, our finances and even our health.

I have a clear line when it comes to dealing with clients' emotions and anger. I tell all my clients up front: "There are two rules: you can't attack you and you can't attack me, besides that, you cannot say or do anything wrong." It is very healthy and necessary to explore angry and frustrated emotions on the page through the alternate handwriting. It is not okay to express anger toward the facilitator. A clear boundary is set here and must be respected. If a client crosses that boundary, then likely the client is not ready to do this work. Any anger pointed at the facilitator is from the conscious mind. When anger is expressed toward the facilitator, the emotion is not coming from the subconscious and has no healing value. The subconscious is completely unaware of the facilitator. Even though the facilitator will be telling the client what to write in the beginning, to the subconscious the facilitator does not exist.

When dealing with wounding, the subconscious is stuck in the time of the traumatic experience or event. It is not in present time and therefore is unaware of what is happening in the client's current reality. Its only concern is the pain that he/she is experiencing in that time. When a traumatic experience happens, time stops. This is the time the subconscious is locked into. This is the time this part knows, at least until it can become unfrozen from that trauma and that time.

It is important for facilitators in training to recognize misdirected anger. As a client begins to *unfreeze,* wounded parts can, and likely will, come up angry with the client personally. They may be angry with them for abandoning them, shutting them away, not paying attention to them, etc. This can be very confrontational for the client. It is important to give that anger a place to be expressed and released. It is tremendously effective and can easily be handled through the alternate writing where it is kept on the page. Understand that this anger has nothing to do with the facilitator. Any anger directed toward the facilitator is misplaced and needs to be put back on the page where it belongs.

THE EMOTIONAL SCALE

Below is an ordered list of human emotions called *The Emotional Scale.* This comes from the Esther and Jerry Hicks book *Ask and it is Given.* At the bottom of the list are the lower vibrational emotions like *fear/grief/ depression* and *powerlessness.* It continues to rise up as if on a ladder to the higher vibrations of *joy/appreciation/freedom and love.*

I have included this list to show the range of emotions we can experience. While some emotions do not appear to be good ones, such as *doubt,* it is still a step up from other lower vibrational states of *blame and worry.* And *anger* is a higher state of being than *unworthiness or depression.* Jumping from *hatred/rage* to *joy* may be a near impossible feat, but with patience and persistence it is very possible to continuously step up to closer, higher vibrational stages on our way to *joy.* Wherever we are on this scale, there is a natural step up that is not that far away. The progress we make is completely individual to each of us; no two people are alike. A step up whether small or large is a success.

In this work, the healing is in the feeling. We must feel the emotion to be able to heal it. *The Neuro Trauma Healing Process* provides us with a safe, supportive place to do that. We can let these states of emotion come out on the page. There they are given the space and permission to be explored in a safe, controlled and loving environment. When we do the alternate writing, it allows the parts of us that are in these states to express themselves completely and receive compassionate support. Doing the work allows these difficult emotions to come out on the page where they will not have a negative effect on our life; where they will not hurt us or anyone else.

1. Joy/Knowledge/Empowerment/Freedom/Love/Appreciation

2. Passion

3. Enthusiasm/Eagerness/Happiness

4. Positive Expectation/Belief

5. Optimism

6. Hopefulness

7. Contentment

8. Boredom

9. Pessimism

10. Frustration/Irritation/Impatience

11. Overwhelm

12. Disappointment

13. Doubt

14. Worry

15. Blame

16. Discouragement

17. Anger

18. Revenge

19. Hatred/Rage

20. Jealousy

21. Insecurity/Guilt/Unworthiness

22. Fear/Grief/Depression/Despair/Powerlessness

DEVELOPMENTAL AGES AND STAGES

The following are the *Developmental Ages and Stages* for a child's development (the basis of which was taken from *Erikson's Psycho Social Developmental Stages*). This is helpful information to gain insight and understanding of what a child may be going through and what their basic developmental needs are at different ages. Please remember, though, that we always get our direction for facilitation directly from the inner child first. We are not trying to lead the Inner Self, we are asking and listening for what they want or need. But in times of confusion or even withdrawal, the developmental chart may be helpful when doing the alternate writing.

A) Infancy – 0 to 18 Months: Trust/Hope

Major Question: *Can I Trust the People Around Me?*

Basic Virtue: Hope

Supporting Environment:

- *I'm so glad you're here.*

- *We're so glad you're a boy/girl.*

- *I want to be with you and near you.*

- *Your needs are okay with me.*

- *I will look after you and meet all of your needs.*

B) Early Childhood (Toddler) – 18 Months to 3 Years: I Can Choose/Try

Major Question: *Can I do things myself, or am I reliant on the help of others?*

Basic Virtue: Will

Supporting Environment:

- *It's okay to explore.*

- *It's okay to leave—be separate.*

- *You can go away and come back, and I will still be here.*

- *You don't have to be in a hurry.*

- *You don't have to worry.*

C) Pre-School Age – 3 to 5 Years: Exploration

Major Question: *Am I Good or Bad?*

Basic Virtue: Purpose

Supporting Environment:

- *I love watching you grow. I'll be there for you to test your boundaries and find your limits.*

- *It's okay to think for yourself.*

- *It's okay to find the difference between boys and girls.*

- *I'll set boundaries for you to help you safely find out who you are.*

D) School Age – 6 to 12 Years: Self-Confidence: "I am good," and "I am good enough"

Major Question: *How Can I be Good?*

Basic Virtue: Competence

Supporting Environment:

- *You can be who you are.*

- *You can stand up for yourself and I'll support you.*

- *It's okay to learn to do things your own way.*

- *You can trust your own judgments.*

- *It's okay to disagree.*

- *It's okay to be afraid.*

E) Adolescence – 13 to 18 Years: Personal Identity

Major Question: *Who am I?*

Major Virtue: Loyalty/Reliability

Supporting Environment:

- *You are free to create/live your life your way.*

- *It's okay and good to explore and find new ways.*

- *It's okay to make mistakes.*

- *You are the source of your success.*

- *You are loved and supported no matter what.*

SOUL FOOD

Within each and every alternate writing session we ask the Inner Self: "Is there anything you want or need right now?" and following through on those requests is an imperative aspect to the *NTHP* process. It is our job to fulfill the promises we make to our Inner Self. These requests and the follow-through is what I have called *Soul Food.* It's a much nicer name than *homework!* And anyway, this is not your average type of homework, because the *work* is obtained through the conversation (alternate writing) with our Inner Self. Whatever we have been asked to do, whatever the task, it will make us feel better. It is what our Inner Self—our Soul—needs. Through *Soul Food* we are essentially *feeding the Soul.*

It may be important to say here, that hurting another or making them feel bad or wrong is never the language of the Soul. Any request to do so comes from a place of disconnection and is not in alignment with higher consciousness and this work. You may feel the need to express anger and hurt, and it is important to do so. This is done solely for the purpose of releasing it from you (and should be kept on the page, or expressed in an *Emotional Release Letter*), not to seek revenge or inflict pain on another. The heart in you is the heart in them; therefore to hurt another is to hurt yourself.

Some people have a very hard time giving themselves what they want and need because somewhere along the way they were taught, or learned, that they were not deserving of having their needs met. This is where we find out if we are willing to show up for our Self – give ourselves what we truly want, need and deserve. And because *Soul Food* is performed on our own, this is where the rubber meets the road. There is no facilitator there to help us with it. By following through for our Self, we can prove that the old way is not true anymore, that we do deserve to have what we want and need to thrive in our life. If we fail to fulfill what has been requested, we affirm and solidify the old belief. With the *Soul Food* we have an opportunity to do things differently and dissolve the limiting belief we have carried with us. Most of the time the part we connect with has been locked away for a very long time, so when you acknowledge them and bring them out of the trauma they have been stuck in, they need your help in integrating into the present time. This is what the *Soul Food* is about—giving them what they need and what they didn't get previously.

The first level of trust is built with our Inner Self by doing the alternate writing, consistently and compassionately. This allows us to align with them. The second level of building trust comes from asking them what they want or need and letting them know that it is now safe and good for them to ask for it. And the third level in building trust is a very important one: to follow through and do what we say we will do—give them what they have asked for. It will be different for everyone. Your Inner Self may ask to go for a bike ride, read a certain book, color in a coloring book, have a nap or take a bubble bath. Regardless of what it is, *do it*. This is critical in the trust building phase. It is how we will learn to believe within ourselves. Some of the things you will be asked to do may sound very simplistic and juvenile. But doing them creates a solid foundation for not only this inner life, but for our understanding that giving to our Self is the very best thing we can do. Over time we will see that serving those needs will come back and reward us handsomely.

Soul Food is given to the client at the end of a session and is discussed with their facilitator at the start of the next session. It is important for the client to write down and follow through on the requests. (Most times it will be only one thing, but occasionally there may be more.)

*Note: Steer clear of making Soul Food into work or a big to do list. The things done for Soul Food are about giving the inner life what it needs to feel safe and good. It should be an enjoyable experience.

There may be times, especially in the beginning, when there is no specific or obvious request from the Inner Self for what they want or need. This may be because they were never asked that question growing up and really do not know. They could also be too afraid to ask, or they are too emotional to put it into words. In cases like these, sometimes their requests are tucked—hidden in the alternate writing—as something like: "Please stay with me" or "I don't want to be alone." If this happens, the *Soul Food* for this person would be to continually (daily) let the Inner Self know that: "You are not alone anymore," and "I am with you—always."

Sometimes, if a person is having a hard time moving into the right brain mode of writing or they are feeling especially closed off to the work, there are certain types of *Soul Food* that can be helpful in opening a person up that does not come from the client's writing. Below is a list of exercises that will help lower resistance to allow the process to flow more easily for them.

*First and foremost, follow the information and guidance given by the Inner Self. These exercises should not come before that.

- Alternate Hand Painting

- Emotional Release Letter

- T.R.E. – Trauma Release Exercise

- Meditation

ALTERNATE HAND PAINTING

The *Alternate Hand Painting Exercise* is used to help people to open up and allow stuck energy and information to process more freely and easily. It is a very simple exercise that is very effective. It is not uncommon for a person to have difficulty allowing the alternate hand to *do its thing* in the writing. The alternate hand painting is a great way to encourage that door of allowance to open. Also, in the early stages of the process, this exercise can be given to keep the momentum up in between sessions.

To do this exercise, take a blank piece of paper or card stock (even printer paper will do), basic paints (watercolors, acrylics, etc.) and a brush. If no paints are available, then the purchasing of the paints becomes a part of the exercise. Use your non-dominant hand to pick the colors. Just like in the alternate writing, let what wants to be expressed come out. Keep your logical, thinking mind out of the way.

Remember, when doing this exercise, it is about opening up and allowing what has been stuck and unprocessed in your nervous system to *loosen up* and come through. It is more about letting go and allowing than it is about *making* something. Don't go in with any ideas or intentions of what you are going to paint, just let your alternate hand pick the colors and paint whatever it wants to. Let whatever wants to come out, come out. It may look like something, it may not—it doesn't matter. The exercise is not about making art, or something we think is good or nice. It is an exercise that allows your subconscious to express in an unpressured and non- threatening, maybe even enjoyable way. It is a helpful exercise to get things moving and flowing, nothing more.

The painting may look like something you understand or recognize, or sometimes it will be squiggles and circles that are completely unidentifiable and have no meaning to you. Many clients find they have drawn people that represent family members, or a representation of the house they lived in while growing up. Sometimes the painting comes out dark and menacing or sometimes there is a sunny brightness; both revealing how the inner life is feeling. However your painting comes out, it is perfect. The exercise is working. The simple act of painting affects thousands of neuro-pathways in your brain. Add the fact that you are doing it with the alternate hand means you are opening up even more pathways—ones that have been potentially blocked.

Note that this painting is not for analysis or critique. If it has meaning to you, fine, but if not, that is fine too. This exercise is helpful in this work because it does not ask anything from this part of us. The inner life can paint whatever it wants to paint, and we will let it. This creates a level of trust and allows for freer and easier expression for them.

One of the most fascinating books I have read in my research of the left and right brain is called *Drawing from the Right Side of the Brain* by Betty Edwards. It is a book on enhancing creativity and artistic confidence and accuracy by teaching you how to truly *see* your subject. Through the drawing exercises in the book, you experience how your brain works—its different functionalities that occur under different sight *perceptions*. She talks about the left brain being the **"great saboteur of endeavors in art"** and shows you how you can access and integrate these different functionalities through the use of the creative right brain.

I needed to provide my readers with exercises that would cause
a cognitive shift to the right hemisphere—a shift similar to that

caused by Upside-Down Drawing: "tricking" the dominant
left hemisphere into dropping out of the task.

~ Betty Edwards

Anne Babchuk, a senior facilitator at *An Extraordinary Life,* has created some terrific tools from the exercises in this book. Exercises that help people who are stuck in logical thinking mode to drop into their right brain, feeling mode and access their expressive, creative side when they are not able to.

I worked with a woman who, during the first two sessions, drew nothing but scribbles and circles in her alternate writing. No legible words were written. Every now and then when we'd ask a question to her Inner Self, a flower would be drawn or something showing us that the inner life was in fact there, and was receiving what was being written to her. This showed me that the level of trust between her and her inner child was very low. The inner life wanted to speak but was too afraid, so it just doodled around and drew a little picture every now and then. To her great credit the woman did not give up on herself and persisted on. Toward the end of her third session she started getting words, and eventually they became sentences. It was then that she discovered why this child was so afraid to express herself.

> *The left hemisphere is the Great Saboteur of endeavors in art. When you draw, it will be set aside—left out of the game. Therefore, it will find endless reasons for you not to draw: You need to go to the market, balance your check book, phone your mother, plan your vacation, or do that work you brought home from the office.*
>
> *~ Betty Edwards*

I speak of this for two reasons. One is that the reluctance of the Inner Self to speak in words or sentences shows us there is a lack of trust and/or fear about speaking and expressing their truth. The fact that something is being put on the page confirms that there is a desire for this Inner Self to connect though. If *anything* comes out, regardless of how small it may seem, it is because this part wants to connect, wants to speak, but is afraid. And two, the simple act of moving the pen (or paintbrush) with the alternate hand makes the process work. This work is certain, it's just a matter of opening up the avenue of allowance and the alternate hand painting exercise is a very effective way of helping that to happen.

If you are dealing with someone who is blocked and seems to continually bring themselves back into the present time, use the yes/no exercise (as described in the *If There is no Response* section) during the writing, and then have them do this painting exercise on their own as *Soul Food*. Have them paint until it feels complete to them. When the painting is finished it is to be put up where they can see it, like on the refrigerator door. It is their child's painting, after all.

EMOTIONAL RELEASE LETTER

The writing of an *Emotional Release Letter* is an exercise to be used when a lot of latent anger, bitterness or frustration has come up in an *NTHP* session.

It can also be used to say something to the person the emotion is directed at, that wasn't said at the time of the event. By doing this, the client brings older, unfinished business to completion. The letter is most often written toward someone specific and significant in our life, usually a parent, primary caregiver or sibling. Through this exercise, the negative energy can be released in a controlled, yet powerful way.

It is important within the *NTHP* process to allow the feelings that come up from the Inner Self to come through and not to block them. With this letter, when we allow them to express freely we can direct this energy to the page and let the emotion come out in a safe and controlled environment. This exercise keeps the emotions from coming out in a destructive way in your life, and from being directed at someone else.

It is rarely given out to people just starting their journey in the process, but only after the connection and trust with the inner life has been established. It can be done more than once, but is usually used only two or three times to let go of the *big rocks* of emotional baggage.

*Note: This letter is only to be written after your Inner Self consents through the alternate writing that **they** want to write it.

The emotional release letter is addressed to that specific person you are angry or have unfinished business with. This person may still be living or deceased, it doesn't matter. Write this letter with the freedom of knowing that you do not have to deliver it to them. Use the dominant hand and write whatever comes to mind. Write without thinking, editing or blocking. This is *stream of consciousness writing* and will allow the emotion to be directed at the page. But note, while it is important to write until the letter feels complete, this exercise should be done in one session. It is not meant to be something a person spends a great deal of time contemplating, planning or going into great detail on. It should not take hours or days to write. Write it quickly—get it on the page. When this is completed, ask your Inner Self, through the alternate writing, if they are okay with what was written and if anything more needs to be said. Make any changes or include any additions that were requested and sign off with sincerity.

When this letter is fully complete, you will likely be very emotional. It is now time to let that emotion go by burning the letter. Find a safe place to do this: outside, over a metal garbage can, in a fireplace, outside on cement, on a rock by the river or what have you. Before you burn it, read the letter over again. Say goodbye to this energy that you have carried for so long. Say goodbye to the way the relationship with this person has been. Say goodbye to the emotional attachment this experience has held over you. Then burn the letter. Watch it burn, see the flames rise into the ethers and turn into nothingness. *Make sure all of it is burned,* leave no corners or bits of writing un-burnt. Make sure it is completely burned through and through. See the ashes, throw or kick them away or flush them down. See that they are gone, that you have fully let it go. Take your time with the burning part of this exercise.

Go back to the page, and through the alternate writing ask your Inner Self how they are doing and how they felt when the letter was burned and let go. Ask them if they want or need anything. Continue with any dialogue that is required, but more than likely, your little one will be tired and want to rest. Take some time to let the effects of this exercise sink in and settle.

The Emotional Release Letter

- Use your dominant hand.

- Write a minimum of one page, single-spaced on lined 8.5" x 11" paper.

- Address the letter to whomever you are angry, or have unfinished business with.

- Write with the freedom of knowing you are safe to say whatever you want to say, and that you do not have to deliver it.

- Write what comes to mind—use *stream of consciousness writing*

- (no blocking, editing or thinking).

- Write until it feels complete and everything you want to say is written down.

- Upon completion *through the alternate writing,* ask your Inner Self if they are okay with what was written, and if there is anything more they would like to say. Let them reply, making the additions or changes requested.

- Find a safe place to burn the letter.

- Re-read the letter.

- Say goodbye to the energy you have carried—how the relationship was and your emotional attachment to it.

- Burn the letter. (Take care to be in a safe place!)

- Throw the ashes (any remnants of negative emotion) away.

- Connect with your Inner Self through the alternate writing again.

- Take some rest.

TRAUMA RELEASE EXERCISE (TRE)

The Trauma Release Exercise (TRE) is a series of exercises and stretches that help a person to physically release trapped energy in their body, energy that comes in the form of tension, stress and past trauma. This is given as *Soul Food* because it is a simple, safe and easy exercise for clients to do on their own at home. It is a good addition to their *NTHP* work, as a non-invasive tool to help them to slow down an over-active nervous system.

The creator of TRE is trauma intervention and conflict resolution specialist, Dr. David Berceli Ph.D. In his book *Shake it Off Naturally* he outlines the technique of encouraging the body's natural shaking response, which both relaxes physical tension patterns in the body and reduces psycho-emotional stress.

TRE targets a very important muscle in our body, the *Iliopsoas* muscle, commonly known as the *psoas*. It is a muscle that is attached to the lower spine and reaches through the pelvis to attach to the femur at the hip. The psoas muscles are the deepest muscles in the core of our body and are the only ones that attach our spine to our legs. Within Taoist traditions, the psoas has been called the *muscle of the soul*, because it resides in the lower *dan tien*, one of the human body's most prominent energy centers.

The psoas has also been called the *fear muscle*. The reason for this is: when we are frightened or under stress the psoas muscle contracts. Because the psoas is connected to the tendons of the diaphragm, it is directly related to our breathing and the *fight or flight* response. The muscle tends to hold within it the tension and energy of these past overwhelming experiences and is hence labeled the *fear muscle*. When we put all of this information together we see that the psoas muscle significantly impacts our functionality both physically and psychologically.

Liz Koch, author of *The Psoas Book*, says: "The psoas is so intimately involved in such basic physical and emotional reactions, that a chronically tightened psoas continually signals your body that you're in danger, eventually exhausting the adrenal glands and depleting the immune system."

Dr. Berceli's TRE Exercise is physically easy to do and allows the body to release the tension held in the psoas in a safe, easy and natural way. The first step of the exercise is to fatigue the psoas muscle through a series of simple exercises and stretches. The next step is to lie on your back on the floor in an easy but specific position. What happens is truly fascinating. The upper and lower legs begin to shake involuntarily, and sometimes the shaking moves up into other parts of the body. It is easy to induce, is painless and, when you get over how odd it is, it feels quite pleasant. This shaking is the body's natural reflex of the nervous system to release tension the same way animals in the wild release trauma from their bodies.

Please remember, in this work TRE is a tool. The most important aspect of *NTHP* is the relationship you build within yourself. Use this tool to help to make that connection easier, more peaceful and powerful. For more information about TRE go to www.reclaimyourpowerprocess.com.

MEDITATION

Meditation is a tool that's sole purpose is to slow down the mind—nothing more, nothing less. It is the simple act of focusing on one singular thing, the benefit of which is phenomenal. Meditation has a lengthy list of benefits, from physical health benefits to the awakening of our senses, that seem to bring us more alive. With meditation we develop a higher degree of awareness that makes our life healthier, easier, deeper, richer and more fun. But one of the most foundational benefits is that it helps to bring us—our awareness—into *the present moment*.

If there was a destination for the *NTHP* work, it would be *this present moment*. When we are in the present moment we are in our *power*. What do I mean when I say *power*? When we are able to slow down our thinking long enough to create a separation from our thoughts, then we are able to have a choice about those thoughts. This ability to choose is *power*. In doing the *NTHP* we are slowing down tapes that have been running rampantly in our nervous system; these tapes are thoughts that some of us have carried our entire lifetime, many of them unconsciously. When we have a meditation practice in coordination with doing the *NTHP* process, it enables us to work both ends of the stick—the conscious and the subconscious. We can do the required inner healing work that slows and stops the internal negative programming that runs as unconscious tapes within us; and with meditation we can practice slowing our conscious mind as well.

There are countless methods and teachings and approaches to meditation. But the first thing to understand is that *there is no wrong way to meditate*. Use whatever way is most effective for you to slow down your thoughts and bring you more into the present moment, at peace. That being said, I have a few tips that can help make meditating easier and a lot more effective for you:

- Schedule *a specific time each day to slow down and still the mind*. If you only meditate *when you get a chance*, or *when you have time*, your meditation practice will most likely be short-lived. It will be frustrating, and you will get very little out of it. It is when you do not have time to meditate that you need to meditate the most. When you slow down the world will slow down with you. To fully experience the gifts of meditation commit to the practice at the same time every day. This builds an association or psychological connection to this time. The body will start to ready itself to slow down regularly at this time, making it easier and easier for you to meditate. *Set yourself up to win. Set an amount of time that you can commit to and will actually do.

- Mornings are great for meditation. The first hour of the day has been called the *golden hour*, because it sets the tone for the rest of your day. This is a good time to meditate because we haven't been sucked into the business of the day yet, and we are more receptive because the mind is still calm.

- It is always a good time to meditate. If we have meditated once in the morning we do not have to wait another twenty-four hours to stop and get peaceful again! Stopping in the afternoon or early evening can be so refreshing, and it is always a healthy and wise thing to do. Especially in this day and age where everyone seems to be in a rush. Slow down, stop throughout the day and get quiet and still. Watch how things will start to *work out* for you, and how you will have more time because of it. All from the simple act of stopping and stilling your thoughts.

- Meditating is like working out at the gym. The more you do it the easier it becomes. Like a muscle, you get stronger with each workout. The ability to slow your mind down becomes easier and easier as you practice. Schedule in your time and just show up, every day. Trust it is working and know that getting frustrated is a trick of the ego. As long as you continually show up with the intention to quiet your mind, you are on the right track.

This next bit of information about meditating is also very helpful to know. The ego—the thinking mind—doesn't want you to slow down! In fact, the ego dies in the present moment and will fight to keep you from slowing it down; in essence, getting rid of it! When you begin a practice of meditation, it is not uncommon to all of a sudden become very busy, with too much to do and no time to meditate. You may find yourself needing to clean up the house, answer that email, make that phone call, take the dog for a walk, etc. … this is the ego's way of distracting you to keep you from stilling your thoughts. When you have this knowledge, you have the upper hand and won't fall prey to the trappings of the egoic, thinking mind.

There are many different ways to meditate. I am going to talk about three primary ways that are used.

Guided Meditation – Many people first start out in their meditation practice using guided meditations. This type of meditation is when you listen to someone who guides you through a series of visual and/or sense-based experiences. This is very helpful because you have something to place your attention on—the sound and direction of their voice. The guide may help you focus on your breathing, get in touch with your body, take you on a relaxing journey to a beautiful destination or perhaps direct you in seeing colors and light. Either way, you are not focusing on your thoughts and are stilling the mind.

Meditating in Nature – Whether you are just starting out or are a veteran meditator, one of the best ways to meditate is to be in nature. By filling your ears with the sounds and by feeling the air on your skin, you focus on natural elements and acclimatize to your own nature. You move out of thinking and just experience nature. But even more than this, being in nature, ideally by water—a running river, a lake, the ocean or a waterfall—you access a very powerful and natural way to come into balance. Have you ever noticed that when you sit by water in nature, even if it is only for ten or fifteen minutes, you leave feeling refreshed? Living in cities and big towns, people tend to become overwhelmed and out of balance from all the cell phone waves, microwaves, power lines and the waves of so many other electronic devices that travel through the air and through the body. When this happens you become over-balanced in positive ions. You cannot understand why you feel *off* or unwell because you do not notice that it is happening or affecting you. Being by water and in nature re-balances you with negative ions, automatically slowing down the mind. Listen intently to the sounds of nature. Not *intensely*, but with your full relaxed attention. Listen into the sounds to the point where it becomes a feeling. A sensation of feeling the waves crash within you, of the stream running through you, of the wind blowing through you. This is how you leave the thinking, ego mind behind and come fully into this moment.

Silent Meditation – The ultimate in meditation is listening to the silence within the silence. You cannot speak and listen at the same time, and thought is simply the mind speaking. If you pay attention to the thinking mind you will see that it won't shut up! It will not quiet until you make the conscious intention to still it. When you do still your thoughts and are beyond them, you will first experience a deeper sense of peace. You will then notice a presence, or a communication beyond words and thoughts where you make direct contact with your higher mind, your higher consciousness. It has been called *the gap, the portal* and *the field*. It is the space between your thoughts. Within this space between your thoughts is great peace, and what occurs from the connection to this space is well-being and harmonious inspiration. There is a conversation or communion going on here that is above the level of thought. This type of meditation can be difficult for some people, especially if just starting out. This kind of meditation does not give the mind anything to *hold on to*, and that can be difficult if you are not used to experiencing silence. So, build your way up to this type of meditating, be patient and gentle with yourself. I have created the *Amplified Silence Meditation (ASM)* that is very helpful for anyone just starting out in this type of meditation. It can also be helpful to long time meditators for taking their meditation practice to a deeper level of connection.

*Go to **www.danestevensonline.com** to get more information about the ASM Meditation, or to use one of the guided meditations there.*

If you are new to meditating, start out with ten to fifteen minutes at a time, and increase five minutes every week or two until you get up to twenty or thirty minutes. You can sit up with your back straight or lay down, whatever is most comfortable and effective for you without falling asleep.

1. Schedule in your meditation at the same time every day.

2. Be in a private, quiet place where you will be undisturbed for the duration of your meditation. Turn off all phones, the radio, computer, TV, etc.

3. If meditating in the morning, make sure you are fully awake. Have your bath or shower first if you like, or simply splash some water on your face to wake yourself up before you start if you need to.

4. Sit with your back straight and your head up. If you choose to lie down, lay on your back with your arms and legs uncrossed (only meditate in this position if you are able to stay relaxed but alert).

5. Close your eyes and focus on your breathing in the start. Take nice easy breaths through your nose, letting them out through your mouth.

6. Stay in a place of relaxed alertness for the duration of the meditation, using the focus you have chosen.

7. Understand that the ego doesn't like, or want to stop thinking, so when a thought does come along, say to yourself: "Aahh, the thinking mind," or "thank you for sharing." Just be aware of it and let it float on by like a cloud, returning your attention back to your meditation focus.

8. Show up every day without fail. Like exercising a muscle, your ability to still your mind will get better and easier as you continue to practice.

LEAVING HOME CEREMONY: GATHERING YOUR CHILDREN

This meditation is performed when you have fully gained *traction*: when your relationship with your Inner Self is consistently positive and healthy in your alternate writing. You can do this step when you have first had at least two weeks of positive connection through consistent daily writing. Please note, it will not be effective if done too soon.

This is a significant step. It is a ceremonial declaration of your independence. You make the declaration by gathering the children of all your developmental ages and stages, saying goodbye to your parent(s) and leaving home. This guided meditation is the stepping-stone that takes you from healing to empowerment. It is the step in which you take over the role of parent and start to become your own source. It is a very powerful realization.

For more information and the full **Gathering Your Children: Leaving Home** – guided meditation, please refer to **Guided Meditations/Exercises** chapter of this book.

*The audio versions of the guided meditations can be downloaded from this site: **www.reclaimyourpowerprocess.com***

YOUR PROFOUND NEW FRIEND

Once you have *untangled* and obtained inner *traction* you will find it becoming easier and easier to follow the guidance from this profound new friend you have in your Self. Information specific to you, for you, will flow easily and naturally. Yes, in the start you will be involved in healing your inner child and inner life. But here is where I must stress that this process is *not* results-oriented. If we have a pre-conceived idea of the direction we want things to go and what we want to do, we end up blocking the natural flow and end up in our own way. When your goal is to create a safe and trusted relationship with your Inner Self, only then will you

When your goal is to create a safe and trusted relationship with your Inner Self, only then will you automatically and easily experience results far beyond what you could have imagined possible.

automatically and easily experience results far beyond what you could have imagined possible.

Your personal guidance system is always there and available to you. It always knows and has your best interests in mind. To follow this path is to be on the path of not only healing, but also freedom and full Self-expression. If you treat this as a journey in Self-discovery you will discover and uncover a person in you that you admire and love. This is the ultimate destination, the ultimate goal, and it starts with connecting within, asking questions, listening and following through on the guidance. Following in this way leads to your true and full Self-expression—to your ultimate Self.

Become a person you admire. Live the life you came here to live. This life is waiting within you to say *yes* to now.

Client Testimonial:

For me, the work was all about the integration of parts of myself that were cast out at a time and age when that was the best, sometimes only, option available. Once returned to my awareness, acknowledged, re-assured and loved with all of the resources I have now, these wounded parts were more than willing to settle down, take their proper place in my memories and stop sabotaging my life.

Part 4

THE GUIDED MEDITATIONS

The audio versions of these guided meditations can be
downloaded from this site. ***www.reclaimyourpowerprocess.com***

RETRIEVAL FROM A PAST TRAUMA - GUIDED MEDITATION

About: This guided meditation is to be used when, through the alternate handwriting, you encounter an inner child or adult in danger, panic, pain or in a state of overwhelm. It is also to be used if your Inner Self asks for help or a hug.

This guided meditation is an important step in stopping an ongoing trauma that continues to trigger and haunt you. What you are going to do in this exercise is go to the subconscious level and literally take the Inner Self out of the experience of the trauma, where it is still going on. When you consciously do that, the trauma simply stops, it just ceases to operate. The wounded part of you will experience leaving the scenario and will therefore accept and know that it is no longer happening.

For this realization to truly sink in, the Inner Self may still need to be reminded a few times through the alternate writing that they are safe, loved, loveable, protected, etc. But after this retrieval, they will likely quickly come back to remembering.

Earlier in this book we talked about how trauma works, but there are things that bear repeating before heading into this exercise. Remember, it is important to suspend all judgment and understand that, to the life inside of you, the trauma is very real and still happening. Be aware that conceptually, that idea is not reasonable to your rational thinking mind.

Also understand that you are not going into this situation cold or without first connecting to that Inner Self and receiving their full permission and expressed desire to do so. You are not forcing this inner life to come with you. Consent is obtained within the alternate handwriting. The retrieval is to be done in an easy and harmonious manner.

Yes, this is a very effective tool for stopping a trauma from continuing to loop within you, **but in order to do this safely, it is necessary to have made a strong connection and have created a high degree of trust with your Inner Self first.** If this has not happened, your Inner Self may not feel safe enough and this carries a risk that the retrieval will not be successful. The connection and trust are established through consistent alternate writing.

To be clear, you are not going to force them out of the trauma or even pull them out of it. You are going to help them by showing them a way to walk safely out of it. This could be considered a form of hypnotherapy, but unlike hypnotherapy, it is only used once the alternate writing has taken you to the point of understanding what is happening for your Inner Self, where they are and what they need. Use this meditation when they want or ask for your help in taking them out of their situation. Do not jump in and take control. There is a possibility of creating more damage and more withdrawal by doing that. Remember, trust is of the utmost importance here; let the Inner Self *tell you* what they need.

*Note: Two meditations are combined here:

- **Guided Meditation for Grounding**

- **Guided Meditation for Retrieval from a Past Trauma**

    *Note: For a first-time retrieval, it is very beneficial to use the two full meditations. (The Grounding Meditation followed by the Retrieval

Meditation.) For a second or third retrieval, or when the client begins to feel more secure and at ease with the guided meditation process, you can use a less time-consuming meditation. You can use a shortened version that still connects them with their body but will bring them quickly into the "field" [see below] to begin the retrieval sooner.

The *Grounding Meditation* creates a feeling of inner support and trust. It also helps to connect the client with their body. It is important that they be in tune and aware of their body and its sensations. This guided meditation can be used on its own to help the client feel safe and become more grounded, or it can be used—as it is here—to prepare a client for the *Retrieval from A Past Trauma*.

Once the client is connected to their body and feeling safe and supported, the facilitator will move into the guided meditation for *Retrieval from A Past Trauma*. This is not *visualization in the ordinary sense*; we are not using the meditation to exert, or even influence what we want to see happen in the event to change the Inner Self. We are only concerned with helping the client to take their Inner Self out of the scene of the trauma. We do this after having expressly received their permission through the alternate handwriting. The facilitator leads the meditation, but interaction from the client is required. The facilitator will ask for feedback at various *checkpoints* and ask the client to describe their interactions with the Inner Self as they move through it.

In the guided visual aspect of the meditation, the facilitator will begin by guiding the client to see himself/herself as healthy and strong, standing in a field. They will take a journey where they will be guided and walked through a series of visual and sense-based locations. This walk will lead them to the place where their Inner Self is having/has had the experience. The pathway there is important because of the left/right-brain stimulation and for what the elements symbolize. Again, the client will need to let go of the need to control and allow this abstract process to take them on this journey from where they currently are to a place back in time where this event occurred. When they arrive at the location they will need to pay attention to what is going on. Let the scene reveal itself to them. They will see their younger self there at that age, at that time. Have them to describe what they see to you.

Facilitator's Notes:

*This meditation will take approximately twenty to thirty minutes. The client should be in a comfortable chair that supports their back and allows them to sit upright with their feet flat on the floor. Make sure the client has some time set aside after the meditation to rest and settle.

*Substitute whatever geography is needed to fit the appropriate landscape for the client. For example, if they currently live in a tropical climate you may choose to use a forest of palm trees instead of evergreen trees.

*In this sample meditation we use the client's home as the destination for the retrieval. Adjust the meditation to arrive wherever the trauma/experience is occurring (school, apartment, field, etc.).

Let's begin.

1) Guided Meditation for Grounding

Make yourself comfortable…

Take a nice easy breath in through your nose…

Let it pour out through your mouth…

Let your shoulders drop and all worry, stress, and thoughts drop away more with every breath out…

This time, feel the breath come in through your nostrils and follow it as it goes down the back of your throat. Breathe in… and let it go…

This time, feel the breath coming in through your nose and follow it all the way down into your lungs. Breathe into your lungs … and let it go…

Follow this next breath as it goes from your nose all the way to the bottom of your lungs this time. Breathe into the bottom of your lungs … and release…

This time, follow the thought all the way into your stomach. Breathe into your stomach … and release…

*Now follow your breath into your lower torso, your sexuality. Breathe in …
and let it go…*

Now take a breath all the way into your upper legs. Breathe in … and release…

*Now follow the breath all the way into your lower legs, down to your ankles.
Breathe in … and let go…*

*Now take this next breath all the way into your feet. Breathe into your feet
… and release…*

*Keep your attention and focus on your feet now. Be aware of your feet flat on
the ground. Feel the support from the floor…*

*Feel your feet supported by the floor, by the building, by the earth. Feel
that support…*

*Go up from your feet to your ankles, to your shins, your calves and your knees.
Feel all of your lower legs, from your knees all the way down to your feet. Once
again feel the support coming all the way up from the floor…*

*Now move into your upper legs, and feel your upper legs. Feel the front and
back of them, your buttocks, your hips, all of your lower torso. Feel the heaviness of this part of your body being supported by the chair. Feel that support…*

*Now go up and feel your lower back and your upper back. Feel your back
leaning against the chair. Feel how it is being supported…*

*Now take your attention all the way up to your shoulders. Notice how your
arms are hanging off your body. Feel your shoulders, the front and back of
your arms, your elbows, your forearms, your wrists, and your hands all the way
to your fingertips. Feel how they are hanging off your body, and how without
doing anything, they are supported. Feel that support…*

*Go up from there to your collarbone and neck area. Feel the back of your neck.
Feel the sides of your neck, and the front of your neck, and your throat area…*

*Go up from there and become aware of your jaw. Now become aware of your
lips. Go inside your mouth and feel your teeth, your tongue, the roof of your
mouth and your throat…*

Now go up from there and become aware of your nose. Go behind your nose and feel your nasal passages…

Go up from there to your eyes. Feel your eyes. Go behind your eyes and feel your eye sockets. Tell them to let go … let go … let go…

Now feel and become aware of your eyebrows, your forehead, your scalp, and go all the way around your head until you come to your ears. Feel your inner ears, and now go down the back of your neck again…

Realize how your head is completely supported by your neck. Feel this support … and let go…

Feel that support in the back of your neck. Follow it down your spine to where you are leaning back against the back of the chair…

Feel the support at your back without your having to do anything. Feel the safety of that support at your upper and lower back … and let go…

Now go all the way down your back and around to where you feel yourself sitting on the chair. Feeling your hips, your buttocks, and your upper legs. Feel all of these parts of you being supported without you doing anything. The support is simply there…

Realize it is now safe to let go. Give yourself permission to let go … and let go…

Go all the way down to your knees, your shins, your calves and your ankles, down to your feet. Feel the full support all the way down to the floor. Feel it there, without you having to do anything. Feel that safety, give yourself permission to let go … and let go…

Return your attention back to your breathing. Feel the air coming in cold through your nose and feel it leaving your body warmed. You are working perfectly…

Now just let your body breathe itself. Realize that you don't have to try to breathe, that you are not even doing the breathing. Acknowledge your breath coming in cold and leaving warmed … and let your body breathe itself…

Follow that breath through your nose once again all the way down the back of your throat and into your lungs...

As the next breath comes into your body find the warm beautiful expansive space in your chest ... your heart. Feel this beautiful space in your chest expand as you breathe into it ... and release...

Take another breath into this beautiful expanse in your chest again. Breathe all the way into the back of your heart this time ... and let it go...

2) Guided Meditation for Retrieval from a Past Trauma

(Link the meditations and continue on.)

As you take another breath into this warm space in your chest, go into it. Follow the breath and go fully into your heart this time...

Go all the way in until you see yourself standing in a beautiful field...

See this lush, green field scattered with flowers of white, yellow, orange and purple...

See your current self, strong and healthy, standing in this field. It is a gorgeous warm day. The sky is blue. The sun is shining. Feel the warmth of the sun on your shoulder and your head as you walk through this serene field...

*Facilitator Checkpoint: Have your client tell you when they are in this place.

The field is big and relatively flat and easy to walk through. You can see rolling hills around it. You may see some birds flying in the distance...

As you are walking through this lush field with all it's beautiful flowers you notice a little further ahead, a little to the left, a wooden arching bridge...

Go over to the wooden arching bridge now...

*Facilitator Checkpoint: Have the client tell you when they are at the bridge.

When you get to the bridge, continue walking on over it. As you go over the bridge, see the river rushing beneath it. Feel the cool breeze of the air from the water on your skin as you walk over…

The bridge comes out onto a nice wide earthen path that leads into a beautiful forest…

Follow the earthen path and walk into the forest. As you go into the forest you see it is a forest of tall, elegant evergreen trees…

As the path enters the forest it starts to veer to the left, follow it. You automatically smell the smells of the forest: the earthen path, the cedar and spruce trees, the flowers and foliage. Smell all these scents of the forest…

As you keep following this path deeper in, it starts to wind to the right. Continue on the path as it winds to the right now…

You begin to hear all the sounds of the forest around you: the birds chirping, the wind rustling in the leaves, and some squirrels playing. Even though the trees are tall, the sun is shining through, turning everything a beautiful golden hue…

Continue walking on this path until it comes out of the forest. Leave the forest and follow this widened path down the distance of approximately two blocks where it turns right, onto a road. Take that road down the distance of approximately ten blocks that takes you to the front of the house where Little You is right now…

*Facilitator Checkpoint: Have your client tell you when they are in front of the house. Ask them to describe what they see.

Now you are at the front of the house. Where is Little You? Is she upstairs, downstairs or on which floor?

Go in to where she is. If she is in a room, give a light knock on the door, and slowly open it and gently enter the room…

Do you see her? Does she see you?

*Facilitator Checkpoint: Have your client describe them. What does she look like? What is she wearing? What is her emotional state?

Go over to her, get down to her level and tell her who you are. Explain to her: "I am you at an older age…"

Tell her you know what she has been through and you are so sorry…

Let her know that she is not alone anymore, that she is safe with you, and you are there to love, protect and look after her from now on…

Let her know that you are there to help. Say anything you would like to say to her now, as long as it is loving and supportive and is not asking her to do anything, e.g.: "I love you and I am very proud of you. You are very special and important to me. I am here to help you…"

When it feels right, ask her if you can give her a hug. If she agrees, embrace her. Stay in this embrace for as long as she wants to. Feel her warmth against you…

If she needs to cry, let her cry. If she needs to cling on to you, let her cling on. Let her know it is ok for her to feel however she feels. You love her no matter what…

Give her whatever she needs to feel safe and looked after. Remember to stay in the embrace as long as she wants to…

Now ask her if she would like to come back with you and live with you in your heart where you can love and protect her from now on, where she will not have to experience this ever again…

You can let her know that she won't be leaving her family and friends. You are just taking her out of this experience and making it so you will always be with her to love and protect her from now on. She will not be alone any longer. Ask her if she would like that…

*Facilitator Checkpoint: Have your client tell you when the child says "yes."

(If the little one is resistant, *let her know she does not have to do anything she does not want to do, she is safe with you, you are fully on her side and she can always come back if or when she wants to.*)

When she says "yes," take her by the hand (if she is an infant you can carry her) and go out the way you came in...

Go back the same way you came, down that ten-block distance, continually checking in with her to make sure she is doing all right. Take the left turn that goes up the two-block distance to the start of the forest path...

*Facilitator Checkpoint: Have your client let you know when they have reached the start of the forest.

Feel the warmth of your little one's hand in yours (or her body against yours if you are carrying her). Make sure she is doing okay and assure her that you are there for her and that she is safe now...

Continue walking with Little You into the forest. See the evergreen forest with its wide earthen path. Follow it in as it winds to the right. Smell the smells of the trees, the foliage and moist ground as you enter...

The path starts to wind to the left now as you go deeper into the forest. You and Little You can hear all the sounds of the forest: the wind gently rustling the leaves on the trees, birds singing, squirrels playing. Follow the path all the way until it comes to the wooden arching bridge...

*Facilitator Checkpoint: Have your client tell you when they are at the bridge.

You and Little You go over that wooden arching bridge and see the water rushing below you as you move into the beautiful field with its lush green grasses and different colored flowers...

It is still a gorgeous warm day and you feel the warmth of the sun on your fronts and your faces as you come into the field. You may see some butterflies flitting about you and Little You as you walk or skip through this lush, green field. Continue walking through the field, going beyond where you originally entered the field...

As you continue on across the field you notice a little further ahead and a little to the left, another wooden arching bridge. Go to the bridge now...

*Facilitator Checkpoint: Have your client tell you when they are at this bridge.

Go over the wooden arching bridge. As you go over you see the water flowing swiftly beneath you. The bridge comes out onto another wide earthen path that leads into another forest...

As you walk into this beautiful forest you see that this time the path veers to the right. Follow this path. Automatically, you smell the smells of the forest: the moist earthen path, the evergreens and the flowers...

Now the path veers to the left. Follow the path as it goes to the left this time. You hear all the sounds of the forest: the wind rustling in the trees, the birds chirping and chipmunks playing...

Continue walking on this path until it comes out of the forest. As you leave the forest, follow this widened path down the distance of approximately two blocks where it turns right onto a road. Take that road down the distance of approximately ten blocks to the front of the house where you currently live...

*Facilitator Checkpoint: Have your client tell you when they can see the house. Have them explain to their little one: "This is where we live now."

Take your little one on a little tour of your home. Show her anything she would like to see, or you would like her to see. Give her the full tour and lead her back to where you are currently sitting in your chair. Have her stand beside you holding your hand or, if she is small, have her sit on your lap...

Ask her if she is ready to come live with you in your heart where she will be safe, loved, looked after, and she will not be alone anymore. Ask her if she would like that...

After she says "yes," cup your hands in front of you in the shape of a bowl, where your little fingers and the knife edges of your hands touch. See all the aura, essence, energy, beauty and love that is Little You go from standing beside you or in your lap into a beautiful energetic ball in your hands. See that happening now...

See all of her innocence, color, emotion, intelligence, laughter, smile, the light in her eyes and all the beautiful essence that is Little You go from standing beside you into being this beautiful energetic ball in your hands…

*Facilitator Checkpoint: Have your client tell you when they can see their little one completely in and as this ball of energy.

When she has completely gone into, and has become, this energetic ball, slowly lift that beautiful energetic ball and carefully press it into your heart. Feel Little You go into your heart…

Keeping your hands on your chest, feel her in your heart. Take a nice breath inward, one that surrounds her in your love. Welcome her into your heart…

Ask her how she is doing. Ask her: "Are you all right?" Feel her answer…

Now slowly take your hands away from your chest, still feeling Little You in your heart. Take another breath enveloping her in your love…

Move your head a little bit, move your fingers and your toes, your shoulders, your arms, your upper body and lower body. Take a nice breath in and slowly come back into the room…

*Facilitator Checkpoint: Have your client describe how they feel and encourage a drink of water if needed.

Then have your client check in with their little one through the alternate writing, to make sure they are well.

With your dominant hand write: Hello Little _____. How are you? Is everything okay? Do you want or need anything? *Then let her respond with the alternate hand…*

Continue the conversation if the inner child wants or needs to.

GATHERING YOUR CHILDREN: LEAVING HOME - GUIDED MEDITATION

About: The *Gathering Your Children: Leaving Home* guided meditation was inspired by and based in part on Dr. John Bradshaw's *Homecoming* meditation. This is an important and required step in our healing journey. Because of the often confusing and obstructive programming that gets passed on to us from our parents, who were more than likely wounded children themselves, many people never fully leave home. They remain stuck in the past trying to, please, get approval from, forgive, or escape their parents, throughout their adulthood. This guided meditation is the step that allows us to separate ourselves from our parents and take charge of our own life.

This guided meditation is a measured step in the progress of our healing, and is only to be done after a person has gained full *traction*. That is to say, the relationship that has been created with their Inner Self is consistently coming up as a positive and healthy one in the alternate handwriting. Do not do this guided meditation too early, only after at least two weeks of daily writing has produced a consistently positive and healthy interaction.

This is a significant step; it is a ceremonial declaration of your independence. You make the declaration by gathering all of your children at their different developmental ages and stages in this meditation; saying goodbye to your parent(s) and leaving home. It is the step in which you take over the role as parent and start to become your own source. This guided meditation is the stepping-stone that takes you from healing to empowerment. It is a very powerful realization, to be sure.

Facilitator's Notes:

*This can be a very emotional experience. Make sure your client has the time to rest and settle afterward.

*Choose the home that had the most significance for your client, the one they spent most of their upbringing in, or what they would call their childhood home.

*The client should be in a private and quiet room where they will not be disturbed or interrupted for at least thirty minutes. They should be in a comfortable chair that supports their back and allows them to sit upright with their feet flat on the floor. Make sure your client has some time set aside after the meditation to rest and settle.

*Substitute whatever geography is needed to fit the appropriate landscape for the client to see the reality of it. For example, if they currently live in a tropical climate you may choose to use a forest of palm trees instead of evergreens trees.

*Note: There are two guided meditations combined here:

- **Guided Meditation for Heart Opening**

  (This is a shorter opening meditation that is used for clients who no longer require the full grounding before starting.)

- **Guided Meditation for Gathering Your Children and Leaving Home**

1) Guided Meditation for Heart Opening

Be in a comfortable, seated position where you feel supported. I invite you to close your eyes...

Take a nice easy breath in through your nose, let it pour out of your mouth, and feel your whole body relax. Feel your shoulders drop and body relax more with every breath out...

This time follow the breath from the tip of your nose, all the way down the back of your throat ... and let it go...

This time, follow the breath all the way from the tip of your nose into your lungs. Fill up your lungs ... and release...

Now follow the breath all the way to the bottom of your lungs and release it out of your mouth. Feel your body relax further with every breath out ... and let go...

Take a breath into your stomach now. Follow the thought into your stomach. Release it ... and let it go...

Now take a breath all the way into your mid-section, your sacral center … and release…

Follow the next breath all the way to the base of your spine, your root chakra … and let it go…

Take another breath into your root chakra at your tailbone. Fill it up … and let it go…

Take another breath into your sacral center, your sexuality … and release…

This time breathe into your stomach again. Follow the breath into your stomach and lower back area. Fill it up … and let it go…

Now find the warm expansive space in your chest, your heart. Take a nice breath into your heart this time. Fill up your heart … and let it go…

Take a breath into the back of your heart this time. Breathe into the back of your heart … and release…

This time go all the way into that beautiful warm expanse in your chest, your heart. Breathe into and go into the middle of your heart now. Stay breathing here until you can see yourself standing in a beautiful field…

2) Guided Meditation for Gathering Your Children: Leaving Home

(Link the meditations and continue on.)

As you take a breath into this warm space in your heart, go into it fully. Follow the breath and go fully into your heart…

Go all the way in until you see yourself standing in a beautiful field…

See this lush green field scattered with flowers of white, yellow, orange and purple…

See your current self, strong and healthy, standing in this field. It is a gorgeous warm day. The sky is blue and the sun is shining. Feel the warmth of the sun on your shoulder and your head as you walk through this serene field…

*Facilitator Checkpoint: Have your client tell you when they are in this place and are seeing this.

The field is big and relatively flat and easy to walk through. You can see rolling hills around it and mountains beyond that. You may see some birds flying in the distance as you are walking...

As you are walking through this lush field with all it's beautiful flowers, you notice a little further ahead, a little to the left, a wooden arching bridge...

Go over to the wooden arching bridge now...

*Facilitator Checkpoint: Have the client tell you when they are at the bridge.

When you get to the bridge, continue walking on over it. As you go over the bridge see the river rushing beneath it. Feel the cool breeze of the air from the water on your skin as you walk over...

The bridge comes out onto a nice, wide earthen path that leads into a beautiful forest.

Follow the earthen path and walk into the forest. As you enter, you see it is a forest of tall, elegant trees...

The path starts to veer to the left. Follow the path around. As you enter the forest you automatically smell the smells of the forest: the earthen path, the cedar and spruce trees, the flowers and foliage. Smell these smells...

Keep following this path deeper in. The path now winds to the right. Continue on the path as it goes to the right...

You begin to hear all the sounds of the forest around you: the birds chirping, the wind gently rustling in the leaves of the trees, some squirrels playing. Even though the trees are tall, the sun is shining through, turning everything a beautiful golden hue...

Continue walking on this path until it comes out of the forest and turns into a road. The road goes down the distance of approximately two blocks and then goes to the right, the distance of approximately ten blocks. Follow this road that takes you to the front of the home where your children are right now...

*Facilitator Checkpoint: Have your client tell you when they are in front of the home. Ask them to describe what they see.

Walk in through the front door now…

When you enter your home you see that it is transformed. The inside of it is now a large circular room that has a series of five doors on the outer wall that go all the way around the perimeter. It is spacious with room between each door. The first door is to the left of the entrance you have just come through with the last door being on the right.

Turn to the left and walk to the first door… Face the door and open it. See your adolescent-self (Thirteen to eighteen years old) standing there… What does he look like? What is he wearing? What is his emotional state? Embrace him and give him a nice big hug. Tell him it's good to see him. Tell him how much you love him, that he is doing great and he should be proud of himself. Look warmly into his eyes and tell him it's time to gather the rest of the children and leave home now, and that you need his help in gathering the other children…

Take him back out into the big room and move further around until you come to the next door on the left. Open that door and see your infant self (between birth and eighteen months old). What does he look like? What is he wearing? What is his emotional state? Pick him up and give him a nice, gentle hug. Look lovingly into his eyes and tell him how much you love him, how glad you are that he is here and that he's safe with you. Let him know you are there to look after him from now on. Carry him back out into the main room, and go down to the next door with him and your adolescent self.

Walk further along until you come to the next door, which is directly across the room from the door you entered through. Open that door and see your toddler self (from eighteen months to three years old). What does he look like? What is he wearing? What is his emotional state? Give the infant to your adolescent to hold. Get down on the toddler's level and give him a nice warm hug… Let him know how much you love and care about him and that he doesn't have to worry, that you will always be there to help him whenever he wants or needs you from now on. Pick him up and bring him out into the main room.

The four of you now move further around until you come to the next door. Open that door. See your preschool self (from three to five years old). What does he look like? What is he wearing? What is his emotional state? Give your toddler to the adolescent to hold. Get down onto the pre-schooler's level and give him a nice big hug... Let him know how much you love him. Tell him that he is a good boy and how proud of him you are. Take him by the hand and lead him out into the big room...

Move further around to the last door on the perimeter, near the one you came in through. Open that door and see your school-age self (between six and twelve years old). What does he look like? What is he wearing? What is his emotional state? Give the pre-schooler's hand to the adolescent to hold. Then, give school-age 'you' a nice big hug. Tell him how loved he is and how much you appreciate him. Let him know that he is more than enough, that he is great and that he can trust himself. Tell him it's time to leave home now. Take him by the hand and lead him into the main room and take the infant back from the adolescent.

Now, you all walk to the first door you came in through. You are carrying your infant, and holding your school-aged self by the hand. Your adolescent is carrying your toddler and holding the hand of your pre-schooler. Lead all the children out the front door of the house to the outside. Everyone turns around and faces the home.

Now, see all of the different developmental ages and stages of your children – all of the children you just gathered and brought outside, in a line from youngest to oldest. See your infant self merge into your toddler self ... your toddler self morph into your pre-school self ... your pre-school self merge into your school-age self ... the school-age self go into the adolescent ... and the adolescent morph into you; leaving just you...

Now choose a symbolic inner child of whatever age you wish. Have that child stand beside you now.

*Facilitator Checkpoint: Have your client tell you whom they have chosen as their symbolic child and have them describe him/her to you.

Your parents (guardians) then come out to the front...

You and Little You stand hand in hand now and say goodbye to your parents. Tell them: "I forgive you for the bad things you've done and the ways in which you failed me. I know you did the best you could" Say to them: "Thank you for what you have given me and the positive things you have done for me." And then let them know, "I will take the job of parenting over from here."...

You and Little You then turn and walk away from your parent(s) and out to the road. See a long, straight road that goes way into the distance. You and your Inner Child then walk hand in hand down this road away from your parent(s) and your old home.

*Facilitator Checkpoint: This can be a powerful point in this meditation and can be a very emotional experience for your client. Be fully present with them to support them if required.

Your parent(s) have come out to the road and are watching you leave. Look back every now and then to notice your parent(s) becoming smaller and smaller as you walk further away. They may be waving good-bye to you...

Keep walking, watching them become smaller the farther away you get, until they disappear out of sight and you can no longer see them behind you...

*Facilitator Checkpoint: Take your time with this. Give this step as much time as it takes to fully leave – until the parent(s) have disappeared out of your client's sight.

Once you can no longer see your parents, follow the road as it goes around a bend to the left. As you round that turn, you see a group gathered ahead in the distance waiting for you. As you get closer you realize that it is all those who have loved and do love and support you in your life. This group may include a spouse, counselor, coach, friend(s), deity, spiritual figure, pet or a higher power...

Enter into their warm, welcoming care. Take some time here, feel the joy, support, caring, light, love and celebration for you that comes from this group. This is your new support group. Bask in, and soak up, the wonderful feelings of connection with these amazing beings who are loving and celebrating you...

Hold hands with, or carry, your little one as you walk, dance or even party with your group down the road, through the forest, over the wooden arching bridge into the field from where you came. As you make your way across the field, take your time and enjoy the feeling of wellbeing. You are headed toward another wooden arching bridge on the other side…

Your support group is right there walking with you, as you all go across the wooden arching bridge…

They accompany you and continue to celebrate you while walking on the path leading through the lush green forest…

Continue walking on this path until it comes out of the forest and turns into a road. The road goes down the distance of approximately two blocks and then goes to the left, the distance of approximately ten blocks. Follow this road that takes you to the front of the house where you currently live…

*Facilitator Checkpoint: Have your client tell you when they are in front of their current home.

When in front of your home, thank and hug everyone and show your gratitude for the loving support they have shown you in your life and for being there with you now. Say goodbye to them for now, and see them all leave happily and lovingly…

*Facilitator Checkpoint: Have your client tell you when they have done this.

You and your child now enter the house. Give the child a tour if that feels appropriate.

Have him stand beside you, holding your hand or, if he is small, have him sit on your lap…

Ask him if he is ready to come live with you in your heart where he will be safe, loved, looked after and will not be alone anymore. Ask him if he would like that…

After he says "yes," cup your hands in front of you in the shape of a bowl, where your little fingers and the knife edges of your hands touch. See all the aura, essence, energy, beauty and love that is Little You go from standing beside you or sitting on your lap into a beautiful energetic ball in your hands. See that happening now…

See all of his innocence, color, emotion, intelligence, laughter, smile, the light in his eyes and all the beautiful essence that is Little You go from standing beside you into being this beautiful energetic ball in your hands…

*Facilitator Checkpoint: Have your client tell you when they can see their little one completely in and as this ball of energy.

When he has completely gone into, and has become, this energetic ball, slowly lift that beautiful energetic ball and carefully press him into your heart. Feel Little You go into your heart…

Keeping your hands on your chest, feel him in your heart. Take a nice breath inward, one that surrounds him in your love. Welcome him into your heart…

Ask him how he is doing. Ask him: "Are you all right?" Feel his answer…

Now slowly take your hands away from your chest, still feeling Little You in your heart. Take another breath enveloping him in your love…

Move your head a little bit. Move your fingers and your toes, your shoulders, your hips. Feel yourself in your body. Take a nice breath in and slowly come back into the room…

*Facilitator Checkpoint: Have your client describe how they feel and encourage a drink of water if needed.

Then have your client check in with their little one with alternate writing, to make sure they are well.

With your dominant hand write: *Hello Little _____. How are you? Is everything okay?* Then let him respond with the alternate hand…

Continue the conversation if the inner child wants or needs to express something.

Client Testimonial:

I was looking for the next step in my spiritual growth and development, and what I found was the missing step.

Part 5

THE FINAL WORD

THE NEXT STEP IN OUR FREEDOM AND SELF-EXPRESSION

When I first started writing this book I had just come through the most intense time in my life. The pain, frustration and confusion I experienced before discovering this work was overwhelming. As I look back, I am truly grateful that I persevered and did not stop myself altogether. The whole experience was hard on many people, not just me. And I have many people to thank for helping me through that time. It was a very challenging experience, but it clearly had purpose and brought me to where I am today.

Originally, I was writing this book for people dealing with trauma and specifically sexual abuse. Having dealt with the effects of sexual abuse personally, I wanted to help the countless millions of people get off that same treadmill of shame that I had been on. But *NTHP* travelled a lot further than I had any idea it would. As I continued to do the alternate writing and follow the guidance that came from it, a whole world I did not know existed opened up to me. After the *big rocks* of my healing had been dealt with, great wisdom started to come to me. Honestly, in the beginning I did not believe the wisdom was real, even though it was coming through me. The specific guidance and truth I received astounded me. This is when I realized the depth of this process. It is not only for those in search of healing, but also for those seeking freedom and spiritual liberation.

I have heard some spiritual teachers say: "Do not bother going into the subconscious mind because it never ends." But in order to come to peace, people with trauma and deep wounding have no choice but to go there. I know I didn't. It is true, the subconscious never ends, but as I learned, it is the gateway to higher consciousness. As we move from healing to accessing our higher consciousness, life just becomes better and better, richer and richer. Through our healing, the way has been cleared to allow new, pure and empowering energy and intelligence to flow. We start receiving guidance and direction specific to and for us, as well as experiencing wonderful synchronicities. The subconscious continues to morph and grow as an innate love and wisdom that lives through us. This is the expression of our Soul, our first order of purpose here on this plane.

When I first heard Peter Levine say: **"Trauma is one of the paths to enlightenment,"** I thought it was a very strange thing to say. But I now see the profound truth in it. Any pattern of high negative feeling or emotion in our life is the universe's way of getting our attention; it is an opening, a gateway to our Soul. Once we make contact with our subconscious and bring the parts of our Self that have *split off* (due to traumatic experiences) back into alignment, we become *whole* again. We no longer have scattered energies and voices running inside us. Instead we become aligned, together, as one.

> *Trauma is one of the paths to enlightenment.*
> *~ Peter Levine*

I have come to realize that the term *enlightenment* simply means letting go of the heaviness, the heaviness that comes from the false belief that we are separate and alone. That is when this inner part of us is *re-cognized*—brought back into consciousness—and remembers. It is like coming home, home to the life within us where we are no longer alone. This relationship becomes the light from which all things stem and become possible for us.

We come home by slowing down the tapes that have been continually running involuntarily within us. This creates space. Space within us equals peace, and peace brings us into harmony with the higher mind in us. Some would say this comes out as luck. It is not luck. It is being on the same frequency as pure positive energy or pure consciousness, which is what makes up all form or matter. When we are connected to pure consciousness, we reap the fruits of the world naturally, as if by magic, because we are connected with everyone and everything.

When you are connected to source, nothing can go wrong

~ Wayne Dyer

This automatically and naturally occurs as *NTHP* transitions into *Soul Re-Cognition*. The *Soul Re-Cognition Process (SRC)* leads us deeper into the essential aspects, or pillars, of our being. When we nurture these pillars, we become more dynamic, clear and confident in our expression. We stop doing things out of need, fear and *having to*. We become motivated by connection, inspiration and desire—doing things that we love to do that brings us into the state of *flow* or effortless effort.

SRC will reveal our passions and talents and our unique way of *out-picturing* and giving these passions and talents. It will allow them to come through us and be given as the gifts we are meant to share with the world. This can be an exhilarating and fulfilling experience, but I would like to make a point here: we have an inherent joy within us that needs nothing to sustain it. Outer purpose is not the cause of our joy; it is the result of uncovering the inherent joy that comes out of the Soul. Our outer purpose is the product of the Soul.

Client Testimonial:

I am so grateful for the pioneers of NTHP. Ever since the first workshop with Dane things began to happen. I didn't realize it until later, but I was letting go of the garbage that had been my previous focus, and that was so freeing. I feel like I am in the zone—all the time! ... this work has allowed me to access my higher Self, any time, all the time. In retrospect, the NTHP allows one deep, spiritual answers to paradoxical, troubling questions in one's life, that make understanding flow and a joy-filled life happen!

YOUR SOUL'S JOURNEY

I have worked with many clients whose stories make my life look like a cake-walk. It takes an incredibly strong Soul to go through what they went through, but they would not have been given or taken on the task if they were not able to handle it. Did *you* take on a big task in this lifetime? Is this why you have experienced what you have experienced? Understand that the lower down you find yourself, the higher your potential is to rise. This is simple physics that applies to life.

The story you have lived and how you have lived it is what has developed the character and characteristics that make you unique. This uniqueness is the fabric of your Soul. Perhaps your experiences were given to you to help you grow, to help you rise and create a great story, a great life. Maybe your trials, challenges and apparent failures have been placed there to point you in the right direction—inward, to find and grow into your unique and Authentic *Self*. From here new needs and desires are spawned. Along with these needs and desires, your unique abilities emerge to be fulfilled in the world.

The word *Desire* originates from a Latin word meaning *of the father*. Now, I am not a religious person, but maybe this is a bit of a clue. Maybe your desires are placed within you for your *Soul* purpose of fulfilling them. Whether it is an issue with your health, wealth, relationships or expression, if you go within and allow the life within you to express instead of trying to figure it out from your thinking mind, the inspiration and action that comes from that connection will fulfill itself in a much more effective and enjoyable way. A way that is custom-made for you. Mentally and emotionally connecting to your Inner Self will perpetuate perfect outcomes. Not just for you, but with a synchronicity that is in the highest and best for everyone!

Your life path, in essence, is your Soul's journey. It is allowing your Soul to express through you, as you. This will come out as a life fully realized and joyfully expressed by way of allowing more of who you really are to come through. This may seem daunting, but in saying "yes" to this higher part in you, you will find that the way becomes a joyful adventure! This higher part in you is already within you as your nature, waiting and wanting to come out. Your job is simply to allow it.

The way of the Soul shows you that you are on purpose and always have been. Even the horrible things you experienced had a purpose, and now you will be able to see this as such. I love that about this work, it makes your life make sense. We hear so often "just drop the past, forget it, it is done and gone." First of all, that is not possible for anyone with a trauma or negative pattern running within them and ruining their life. Secondly, this is your life! It has not been an accident. Yes, this infinite intelligence knew what she was doing with your life! Your life is an amazing story. Do not drop the past. It is what brought you here to this point in your life: to the realization of your Inner Self, to the recognition of your Soul. When you heal the negative parts of your past, you will be able to look back upon and smile at an amazing success story of healing and growth.

When we were going through it, at the time it seemed like complete chaos, but as I look back now, I see how perfectly orchestrated it was.

~ Joe Walsh

YOUR INNER GUIDANCE SYSTEM

You are now on the threshold of the relationship that is the foundation of all of your other relationships, the one with your own personal, inner-guidance system. It is the animating principal guiding you to living your ultimate life. Give yourself the credit you deserve for embarking on this journey. This is brave work, not for the faint of heart, and you are doing it. However, you cannot skip steps. If, through this process, you are willing to go into the FEAR *(False Evidence Appearing Real*—the erroneous belief in separation that is the very core of the human condition), you will see through the illusion and recognize the dysfunctional pattern as the opportunity that it is. It is an opportunity to re-cognize; that is, bring all of you, who you really are, back into this present moment, back into consciousness.

You will find the inner relationship you are cultivating will become your trusted guide that will always steer you in the right direction. You may sometimes have a different idea, want or even a fear of the guidance that comes to you, but you will learn that it leads you down the best possible path for you. When you allow and follow the guidance this innate wisdom has for you, it will inevitably lead you to a far better outcome than you could have predicted if you were trying to orchestrate it from your thinking mind. You will also come to learn that if you do not follow that guidance and let your energy flow, there is a very good possibility that things will not turn out for the best. Don't worry, living life from this place is very forgiving. Be patient with yourself, in this new way of being in and with the world.

YOU BECOME YOUR SOURCE

My goal in writing this book was to have you receive the relief and healing you need, but also to help you understand your power. When you come to inner harmony, connect to your inner life and become whole, you will find yourself relating to a higher wisdom than you have known in your life before. This wisdom and knowing is accessed inside you and is a part of you. As you build this relationship you will come to know that it is always available to you, and you will learn to trust and use it more. Over time you will know you can rely upon this intangible presence as your source. To become your own source is true power and the ultimate in response-ability.

When you realize you are always affecting your world, that you are in fact a creator, you will soon come to understand that you *are* your own source. You will then stop looking for your good, your supply, your acceptance, worth or love from people and things outside of yourself or in your thinking, and instead go within. You understand clearly that the inside creates the outside, and if you cannot give it to yourself within, then you cannot get it *out there*. You have become fully *response-able* and reclaimed your power—the mastery of your life.

What if the world was simply a feedback system showing you what you are thinking, what you are believing and how you are treating yourself...

MOVING FORWARD

This work travels a very long way. It moves from healing your past and bringing it to resolution, into personal power and spiritual liberation. Because of this, I felt it would not be fitting to write the entire distance of it in one book.

This natural evolution goes from doing the *NTHP* healing work into the empowerment aspect of the work we call *Soul Re-Cognition (SRC)*. The next book, *Unleash Your Genius*, is the guidebook for *SRC*. It reveals the next steps of this process that will propel you forward into becoming fully Self-expressed in the different fundamental aspects of your being:

- **Wisdom**: Clarity, Connection, Purpose and Direction

- **Love**: Beauty, Sensuality, Relating and Allowance

- **Creativity**: Manifestation, Curiosity, Play and Transformation

- **Power**: Strength, Will, Integrity and Movement

You come into balance and become fully Self-expressed when these four spokes of the wheel of life are even. When you are fulfilling all the wants and needs of these aspects of you, the wheel of life rolls smoothly. As you fulfill this balance, you create more space and aliveness within you and you will feel stimulated and inspired. This balance brings you into the state of effortless effort, known as *flow*.

With *SRC* you will learn about who you are in a profound new way—from the inside out. Until now, most of your information about who you are has come from outside of yourself. As you have experienced through the *NTHP* work, you have been *trained* in how you are to be by your parents, your upbringing and by society. How crazy is that?! When you embark on the *SRC* work you will receive specific information about yourself for yourself, from your *higher* Self — information about what you need to feel good and become fully Self-expressed in all areas of your life, as well as to become aware of your place in the world.

> *You are a spiritual being having a human experience*
> *to reveal your divinity.*
>
> ~ *Michael Beckwith*

It may seem like a quantum leap from doing inner child work to such an evolved practice, but you will see it is a natural and seamless step from the *Neuro Trauma Healing* to the *Soul Re-Cognition* work. If you have done the work in this book and have come to a place of consistent, positive *traction* with your Inner Self, then you are ready for this next step.

THANK YOU

You are very brave to embark on this inward journey of healing and alignment. This work has the potential to be the most rewarding and life-changing you will ever do. I assure you this *work* will turn into great joy, not the kind of joy that is a fleeting search for happiness done in an external effort to make yourself feel good. This is a deeper, self-sustaining joy that is founded in peace. This joy is always alive within you and does not need anyone or anything outside itself to exist. It does not come via artificial stimulation, stimulation that makes you feel on top of the world for a short period of time only to leave you feeling empty after the excitement has worn off, the toy or the person is gone, or the event is done. It sees the externals as wonderful gifts to be enjoyed and played with, but not something you need to attach yourself to in order to feel good about yourself, to be happy, fulfilled or loved.

There is a constant joy within that needs no stimulus.

~ Joel Goldsmith

To live in a true state of peace is to allow the free flow of this living life to flow through you without the need to hold on to people, personas or things as a part of your identity. The real truth is that the world can only be a friendly place if it is a friendly place within you. The world can only be a loving place if it is a loving place within you. You are the main contributor to the life you are living. Your energy, thoughts and emotions are creating how you experience your life. They are also contributing to the collective consciousness that affects everyone else too. Yes, you are the director of your life, but you are also a very important contributor to the world.

Your alignment with your Soul is your highest contribution to the rest of the world.

You are contributing to this collective consciousness whether you are aware of it or not. It is the primary energy field that touches and impacts everyone and everything. By doing your inner healing work you are changing your energetic deposit and are becoming an integral part of bringing long-standing patterns of pain and dysfunction to an end; first within you, and then in the world. In other words, you start depositing positive, loving energy instead of fearful and anxious energy into the collective consciousness.

Trauma is getting a lot of attention these days. We are now starting to realize just how many *negative outcomes* (addiction, heart disease, depression, obesity, etc.) originate from negative and adverse experiences that are trapped in the body as trauma. We have not known how to deal with this stuck energy and have passed these dis-eases and dysfunctions on to our children. It has become a runaway train cutting a swath of destruction through society, with pain, frustration and dysfunction turning into crime and violence. As the population grows, more trauma and dysfunction are being passed on. We do not talk about our thinking and mentality as being a tangible thing, but our energy, thoughts and emotions have a direct effect on everyone around us. Fearful, angry or negative energy is mental pollution that spreads like a disease.

That being said, thank you for being brave enough to step up and do your inner healing work. The time has come to stop the vicious and cruel cycle of passing on the pain and dysfunction that originated from our ancestors. The only place where we can start is from where we are, and the only way we can stop the cycle is by stopping it within us. Once healed, we no longer have the pain, anger, shame or dysfunction within us to pass on. We are no longer triggered or reactive to external events. We have stopped being a part of the problem and have become the solution. Doing this depth of work makes you a leader—a hero, if you will. Your light will automatically begin to shine and illuminate the darker places in your life. Your light will also positively affect other people and have a healing effect on those you come into contact with in your world.

One candle lit lights another.

This is the start of turning the tables on mental health. It directs the momentum back to our nature of safety, peace, playfulness and love. These characteristics are our nature, we do not have to do anything except get out of our own way to have them. They are a part of our makeup. They are our birthright.

Let the flame of awareness that has been ignited in you spark others to awaken to the peace and the magic within them. A single spark has the potential to set a forest ablaze.

Heal your past, ignite your gifts, passions and purpose; live the magnificent life you came here to live, by simply being who you really are.

With great love and gratitude,

Dane Stevens

CLIENTS' STORIES AND TESTIMONIALS

These are true-life stories and testimonials. Express consent has been given to share these stories, but to ensure the protection and privacy of the client, their names, the places, and anything that might identify them has been changed within the stories.

Lynn's Story: PTSD

As a baby, Lynn was shuffled from house to house while her mother worked excessive hours. She was neglected and left alone in her crib for long periods of time. At two years old she became unresponsive, refused to eat, and became life-threateningly thin. Lynn's aunt, who was looking after her, said the doctors did not think she would make it. Her survival is credited to bonding with a dog that was placed in her crib by her desperate caregiver.

Lynn was also exposed to alcoholism and abuse at a very young age. By the age of eleven, she began working seven days per week. A typical workday was from 4 a.m. – 11 p.m. By the time she was fifteen she was so weak and thin that the doctor wanted her hospitalized. She continued this grueling, abusive schedule into her adulthood. She developed an eating disorder and through her twenties and thirties battled with anorexia and bulimia.

Lynn began to experience PTSD at sixteen after she had a particularly charged traumatic encounter with a man who attempted to strangle her. For over forty years, the PTSD had caused her to jump and yelp every time someone came up behind her.

Lynn experienced many different traumas and abuses growing up and the unprocessed energy of these experiences out-pictured in many dramatic ways in her adult life. By the time Lynn had found the *NTHP*, she was desperately ready for change.

Lynn's Testimonial:

I would like to share my experience with you regarding this healing process.

Initially, I was very skeptical of this process and if it would be of benefit for me. Over the span of forty years I had tried so many types of therapy from the conventional to the unconventional. I wasn't sure if yet another attempt would be of any use for me, not to mention the expense I had spent over the last decades. Was I willing to try yet again?

I am so extremely grateful that I did continue on.

Noticeable changes in my life have included:

- *I am no longer reactive to forty-five years of dealing with PTSD. That statement alone is life-altering. Family, friends and colleagues have noted the remarkable changes.*

- *Since earliest childhood, I had what I thought was a physical limitation. I was unable to take any deep breaths. It did not even occur to me that this was something that could have been from an emotional trauma. I had the assumption it was just my lung capacity; it was just smaller than normal. It may seem a simple thing to anyone else, but to be able to breathe deeply and freely is immense. From this alone, I am more relaxed and can sleep more deeply.*

- *I have more self-confidence, and I feel empowered. I am engaged and more relaxed in my life, including being with my family, friends and colleagues.*

- *I have opened up to an inner world that I did not think was possible. I have struggled with any type of writing, journaling, and envied those that could do so. It is to my greatest astonishment and delight that I can participate in writing which is so profound.*

I am in awe with the compassion and integrity of my facilitator as I was guided through my process of healing.

Deep healing is possible; do not hesitate to immerse yourself!

Ken's Story: *NTHP* and the Heart

Ken was a young forty-five-year-old. He rode his bike, did yoga, played hockey, traveled and was often up for a good night of dancing. He seemed completely healthy and in good form, so when he contracted a heart issue it completely blind-sided him. An irregular heartbeat had the doctors concerned, and he and his wife even more so. Over the course of ten years he had electro cardioversion thirty-five times and had three ablation surgeries that helped him temporarily, but his heart continually returned back to the irregular and inefficient rhythm that left him short of breath, out of energy and in an anxious state knowing the next attack could be at any time. The next step in the journey was a pacemaker.

When Ken found out about the *Neuro Trauma Healing Process*, he was in a place of high anxiety. He was scheduled to have another heart procedure; it was a final attempt to calm his heart. Being a successful entrepreneur, Ken's time was precious to him, but with what was on the line, he made the time to do the work.

It took him two months to do his inner work. He was committed and worked diligently. In that time, and just prior to his procedure date, his heart was in permanent arrhythmia. He did have the procedure, but it was unsuccessful. He was given electro cardioversion, sent home, and was advised he would be booked for the pacemaker procedure.

He was in anxiety awaiting the return of the symptoms when a calm came over him, the anxiety disappeared, the arrhythmia did not return and so the doctors delayed the procedure until it re-occurred. That was in November of 2013—it has never returned. Ken's energy levels are back to normal, and his breathing is full and steady. He is now back riding his bike, doing yoga, playing hockey and frequenting the local jazz scene yet again.

Ken's Testimonial:

I am a logic-driven person so I am not going to say "miracle," but I will say this: I have had a regular heartbeat for seven months now. (Written in June 2014 and still going strong.) I am impressed and hopefully you will be too. The experience of doing the NTHP work is fascinating, illuminating, spiritual, heart wrenching and somehow enjoyable.

Petra's Testimonial: Chronic Pain & Depression

In 2009 I was in a car accident and severely injured. It left me severely disabled for four years until I could get proper treatment for my brain injury. As a result, I had a mental health breakdown. I experienced clinical depression and went through a lot of therapy. When I came to the NTHP, I was still experiencing pain and terrible headaches. I was irritable—especially with my daughter—and withdrawn from socializing. I had great difficulty concentrating and had a hard time getting simple, daily-life things done. Also, I would experience great anxiety driving over the bridge where the accident happened. I would pass the spot at least two times a day, and the anxiety was terrible.

After my first introductory session, I knew immediately that NTHP was for me.

This work has been huge for me, and I am blown away that the guidance (for my healing) came from within me. This alone was very empowering. After only the second session, my headaches drastically reduced. I am no longer popping pain pills and am sleeping without the aid of them. I am a much happier and relaxed person, and my daughter tells me how nice I am now! My concentration is so much better, and I am able to keep on top of the household chores. I am socializing more and am making many new friends... Oh! And, it seems my attraction light is lit once again!

One of the most effective things my facilitator took me through was a guided meditation in which I walked away from the accident. My anxiety is completely gone, and I can now pass the accident site without being triggered, and really, I am now a much better and confident driver.

I am blown away by the deep wisdom I have within me, and I have gained much clarity as to the root causes of many issues. I received amazing clarity on beliefs I had running within me about my identity and my contribution to many of the negative events of my life.

Everybody who goes through any sort of therapy, especially for clinical depression or the effects of an accident, 100% definitely should engage in this work.

I really loved my facilitator; she was very compassionate and really "with me" through it all. She helped me to see what I was telling myself!

It is amazing what you can do for yourself by going through this process, and it is amazing the healing you get from it. Outstanding, well worth it!

Tamara's Story: Childhood Sexual Abuse

Like many, Tamara came to NTHP out of necessity. She was in an abusive relationship that she knew was bad for her but could not end. It was a scenario she had experienced before. She was seeing the destructive pattern in her life of abusive relationships and self-sabotage that she desperately wanted to put an end to.

Through the work, Tamara made contact with a deeply-rooted experience that had created a sense of self-loathing and shame within her.

Tamara was raised in a large religious family. They were a close and loving bunch. Extended family lived close by and large family get-togethers happened frequently. At one such gathering, when Tamara was six years old, her older, twelve-year-old cousin touched her sexually. She looked up to and trusted him and since he hadn't *hurt* her, nor was *mean* to her, she did not see that what happened was inappropriate behavior.

Each time the families got together, her cousin continued this behavior, and his sexual promiscuity escalated and became more advanced with each encounter. Tamara did not want to disappoint him or get him into trouble, and he would confuse her by being nice and giving her candy. She instinctively knew the families would be *devastated*, so she continued to go along with it and told no one. This went on for a period of almost two years, until she got up enough nerve to tell him to stop and began to completely avoid him at the gatherings.

But as Tamara grew up she felt a great deal of shame around the experiences, for both her participation and her silence. She tightly packed these experiences away, but the energy was always pushing to come out and in fact did—uncontrolled in the form of the destructive patterns she was experiencing as an adult.

With *NTHP*, Tamara was able to let the energy of the experience out of her body. She allowed the wounded little girl inside to speak up, and as she did, Tamara learned how to support and show compassion toward herself through it. Tears flowed readily, and she was able to forgive herself for letting her cousin take advantage of her and for not letting this inner part of her speak up about it. *She could look herself in the mirror again.*

Once this inner transformation took place, other things fell into place easily. Tamara was able to speak and find closure with her cousin. She was able to forgive him as well. Slowly but surely, the abuse of her current relationship subsided and in time she ended it for good. She signed up for the schooling she needed for her dream job and is now moving forward in life with peace and confidence toward a bright future.

Tamara's Testimonial:

The Neuro Trauma Healing Process *has completely freed me from my past. I have been dealing with sexual abuse for the better part of my adult life. I have done a lot of counseling for it, but I never got anywhere with it. I would just shut down, and it wasn't effective for me. I've never experienced anything like this* (NTHP) *before. This work took me to a place I've never been in my life, and honestly didn't think I would be able to get to … Today I have a big smile on my face because I don't live in the past anymore. I really didn't realize I could have this kind of freedom. I'm not stuck and frozen anymore. I'm finally able to start progressing in my life again! It feels like a fog has been lifted. I'm excited about my life now!*

Jenna's Story: Addiction

Jenna was raised in an alcoholic home. She experienced ongoing emotional trauma throughout her childhood and teen years. She herself became an alcoholic, drinking daily by the age of fourteen. At twenty-four, Jenna did what it took to become sober, but she continued to carry many of the self-defeating beliefs brought on by growing up in an addicted family. She did not feel worthy. She felt she had to sacrifice herself to be liked. She walked on eggshells with everyone, terrified to disappoint them, and she spent most of her life *stuck*. Physically, Jenna developed arthritis and was in pain every day.

By the time Jenna turned forty-three she was divorced and raising two children as a single parent. She had accumulated a substantial education and had a tremendous amount of life experience but found herself stuck in a job she hated. She had big dreams but was terrified to take the leap. Jenna needed help but had no idea how to find it.

Jenna's Testimonial:

I was stuck. I'd been stuck for years and had no idea how to move forward. I went to the West Coast Women's Show and literally found Dane and Anne. I was drawn to their booth and even said that day to Dane: "I don't know why I am here, but I am." I signed up for the introductory sessions figuring "what did I have to lose?"

I did the first session and noticed a difference immediately. It wasn't tangible, but it was something. I kept going and, after my third session, I couldn't wait to do more. I don't know how many sessions I have done anymore because I have taken over the work for myself and NTHP has become part of my daily life.

Here is what I know...

- *I have more confidence. So much so, I took a huge risk and am a contributing author of a best-selling book.*

- *My private practice is flourishing, and I love my work so much it doesn't feel like work.*

- *I am no longer stuck in a self-defeating job.*

- *I am no longer in constant pain with my arthritis. I still have challenging days, but nothing like before. (And I'm not done healing yet!) I have become conscious of when I have a flair-up—it means there is something going on with me emotionally.*

- *My ex-husband and I are now on friendly terms, and we are raising our children together. Our relationship was one of the most contentious I had in my life.*

- *My dad is no longer my enemy. Nor does his behaviour hurt me. I can be the best daughter I can be without sacrificing myself.*

- *I believe I am worthy, loveable and don't have to sacrifice myself anymore.*

- *I give to others because I want to, not because I should.*

- *I have a voice and don't struggle to express myself to anyone.*

NTHP changed my entire way of being. I still write almost every day, and I am still growing. I take what I learn through my writing and put it into practice.

NTHP has made such a difference in my life that I wanted to share it with the rest of the world. I have taken the facilitator training and am completing my practical training now. I can't wait to help others learn how to help themselves.

You are reading this because there are no mistakes. Please give yourself the opportunity to immerse yourself in the process. Your life can only get better.

Pete's Story: Neglect

Pete grew up in a very small, remote village in Poland. His family was extremely poor, even compared to the other families that lived in this far-away region. He was born in a one-room house and lived there with his sister, mother, and grandmother. When Pete was still an infant, his mother went to live in the city and he was left in the care of his grandmother. When Pete was five, his mother returned and took him back to live with her. He was taken out of the only home and environment he had known, away from the security of his sister and grandmother, into the big bustling city to live with his mother and her new husband, whom he had never met. It was a shocking experience for a little boy and the first years were not easy on him. At school he got into fights, and at home he spent many lonely, homesick nights.

Through his life, Pete felt anxious most of the time. In looking back, he described himself as *needy*. He tried to cope and cover up the feelings that came from his extreme and volatile upbringing through the bravado of rough sport, fighting and, in later years, through alcohol and drinking excessively.

Pete managed to cope quite well through his life. He quit drinking and helps many others cope with addiction and stay on the straight and narrow, too. But he was never completely free of the past. He was still triggered and reactionary in certain situations, especially around intimacy and relationships. All the work he had done to better himself made him aware of his *story* and he knew healing from his past was the key to his recovery. Only he did not know how until he found *NTHP*.

Pete's Testimonial:

The old kind of advice we would get was: "It was a long time ago, just deal with it and get on with it." And frankly, that hasn't worked for me. I've done fine, but there were these things that were holding me back in terms of behavioral issues and how I react in certain circumstances, especially in intimate relationships.

I just completed twelve NTHP sessions and it's been amazing. As a result of the process I feel much calmer, more alert, more present in the moment, and any fear or anxiety that was lurking in my psyche is gone. What's most significant is the feeling of neediness is no longer there.

What I learned, and actually knew intellectually, was that I had to heal myself, but I didn't know how. This process has shown me how I can do that—and it works. It helps you to not just deal with your issues, but to heal them totally, to bring them home and have them disappear. In twelve sessions I feel like a different person.

I've been doing a lot of inner work for a lot of years, and helping others with other programs, too. And for me this is like homecoming—something I've been looking for forever and finally found it.

Client Testimonial:

I have had many different types of counseling over the years for chronic pain, trauma and fears of all types. I would tire of the same stereotype sessions and in the last few years I have refused to go through the process even though I was offered them for free. But when I saw the NTHP *presentation something clicked. I knew I had to try it. The insights and healing I received were remarkable, and I am very appreciative of all that the process has done for me. I would suggest if you feel a need to be free of all the hurts and pain that you are going through, ask for help and sign up!*

Client Testimonial:

What a powerful way to untangle the pain from the past with gentle loving support and release that pain with compassion and ease!

Client Testimonial:

…these parts of myself are gradually ceasing to be disruptive in their function and are instead joining forces to rebuild what it is that I am truly meant to be.

Client Testimonial:

I feel I have gone through an amazing transformation, and I finally have some balance back in my life.

Client Testimonial:

Wow, it's astounding how much energy you have when you stop feeling guilty and stay tuned in to your Inner Self! It's so incredibly amazing to live in the present, enjoy my work, enjoy the smallest moments every day, and watch the magic of life unfold before my eyes. I am now plunging into the unknown, free from past fears and doing what I always wanted to do … The game of life is no longer difficult—it's fun!

Client Testimonial:

Since my sessions, my life has become richer and fuller. I am present and experiencing joy at work and with my family, and I love the connection blossoming with my daughter. I am especially excited by the option to create my day and my life each moment.

Client Testimonial:

...then all of a sudden, through the NTHP I was able to let go of all the past hurts and wrongs that happened. It's all gone and I'm freed up and am not frozen anymore. My outlook on life has turned around. I've got my courage back and my direction back, and am back in action instead of being frozen.

Client Testimonial:

The work led me to a tremendous amount of power. The depression left, the anxiety left, the resentment and anger, once I could see what the root cause of that was, has disappeared and I don't react with anger and resentment anymore.

Client Testimonial:

NTHP is a very beneficial tool to use in the process of guiding clients to a place of personal awareness and connectedness. I highly recommend this mode of therapy to others in the field.

ACKNOWLEDGEMENTS:

I would like to thank the many people who helped me through my wild ride of healing as well as acknowledge those who helped me put this work to paper and make it available to those who need it. As the saying goes: "It takes a village," and I am very fortunate to be surrounded by many great villagers!

First of all, I want to thank my mother, Ruth Stevens, for being there for me as I went through the vast changes I did not understand, and for her loving support when I was not sure I could handle them. Thank you for being the example of unconditional love in my life and in the lives of so many others. Thank you to my brother, Jim Stevens, for being there to help without a word—even when so much could have been said. And to my sister, Carolyn Lutz for trusting me enough to be a part of this work. And I want to acknowledge my late father, Albert Stevens, for his courage, his strength, and for showing me how much a person can change and grow, despite their past.

I thank Hazel Williams Carter for understanding my journey, for teaching me about trauma and for helping me to forgive; Ida Kendall for her heartfelt teachings and generosity; Mary Hoffman for her incredible selflessness, for spending hours in service to me, ensuring I made a safe and gentle inner connection. I would also like to thank Dr. Peter Levine for his committed study and practice in the field of trauma and for helping many people like myself to understand it with more clarity. And a special thank you to the late Dr. John Bradshaw for his service to those who suffer from abuse, and for his book *The Homecoming* that introduced me to a life of inner connection.

Many heartfelt thanks to Paul Larosa for being such a great and talented friend. *Thanks, Cabana Boy!* for all the Evian, and for bailing me out technically over the years. Thank you Tony Commacho from The Gateway, and Heidi Marie for your friendship, support and encouragement. Thank you Dr. Shelly Bosten for your healing abilities, your intuition and for reminding me of who I am and what I am here to do. To Solvei McKenna, thank you for our Soul's journey that was a significant catalyst for the discovery of this work. Thank you Bob Goddard, Esther van der Werf and the rest of the Full Circle Farm for letting me be a part of the family; Dr. Leroy and Mac Perry of The International Sportscience Institute, for being so accommodating and flexible; Mark Jarboe, Marv Cranston, Sophia Kuzia, Laura DiPietro and Jackie Schreiber for being such supportive friends. Thank you all!

A big thank you to Terry Babchuk and Chrissy Babchuk—your help with the manuscript was invaluable! Thank you also to Luciano DiMarino (*and clan!*) for believing in me and this process and for urging me to bring this work forth fully; Joseph Roberts of *Common Ground Magazine* for his advice on writing, Constance Kellough for offering her knowledge so unselfishly and connecting me with the Unity Spiritual Centre and many great people there; and Barbara Dempsey for being so kind in sharing insights about the biz with me.

I would also like to recognize some of the spiritual teachers that have helped and supported me along my path. They are all a part of this work: Rev. Carol Carnes for being my first guide and teacher; Rev. Kenn and Deb Gordon and the Kelowna CSL for the hospitality to both me and this work; Dr. Michael Beckwith and the Agape Spiritual Center for inspiring and insightful teachings; Eckhart Tolle, who continues to be a staple of my spiritual diet; Deepak Chopra, whose writings have been a constant companion; Esther Hicks for helping me to remember when I forget. And to the countless other teachers, guides and healers that have been a positive and uplifting influence in my life, I thank you.

I want to acknowledge my best friend and my love, Anne Babchuk. Thank you for all the hours at the beach and at home—reading, re-reading and re-working this manuscript with me. Your support and patience has made this book not only a reality but also one peeple kan axually unnerstan.

Thank you, not just for the many long hours you put in, but for the heart and Soul that went along with it, for trusting and taking a leap of faith with me. You are a significant part of this teaching, this book and of me. Thank you Annie B!

Last, but not least, I want to thank all the courageous people who have been brave enough to look inside themselves and do the inner work outlined in this book. You are pioneers on the leading edge of healing and spiritual development. What you have done is significant not only for you and your loved ones, but to everyone you come into contact with, thus, society as a whole.

A special acknowledgement goes out to those who have allowed me to put their story of healing in this book. (Names, places and details have been changed for privacy reasons, but you know who you are!) The space/peace that you have created within you is an opening that other Souls can now come through more easily—to heal and circulate safe, loving and playful energy into our world. Thank you all.

REFERENCES

Anthony, Carol K. *A Guide to the I-Ching: Concept from the 11th Hexagram (Stow: Anthony Publishing Co., 1988)* 50

Barbash, Elyssa. *Different Types of Trauma: Small 't' versus Large 'T',* Tampa: Psychology Today (https://www.psychologytoday.com/ us/blog/trauma-and-hope/201703/different-types- trauma-small-t-versus-large-t)

Belfontaine, Karen. *Portfolio – Avocado Communications* (http://www. avocadocommunications.com/portfolio-karen-belfontaine- therapist.php)

Berceli, David. *Trauma Release Exercise* (https://traumaprevention.com/ about-dr-david-berceli/, 2018)

Bradshaw, John. *Homecoming: Reclaiming and Championing Your Inner Child (New York: Bantam Books, 1990)* 82 -105, 122-140, 157 - 169

Brodal, Per. *The Central Nervous System: Structure and Function, 3rd Ed. (New York: Oxford University Press, 2004)* 369–396

Dilts, Robert. *Reflections on September 11. Santa Cruz* (http://www.nlpu. com/Articles/Sept_11.html, 2001)

Edwards, Betty. *Drawing on the Right Side of the brain, 4th Ed.* (New York: Penguin Group, 2012)

Erikson, Erik, H. *Childhood and society* (New York: Norton, 1950)

Gibson, Ty. *Digma: Episode 11 Frederick's Experiment* (http://www.digma.com/fredericks-experiment/2015)

Gillon, Ewan. *Person-Centered Counseling Psychology: An Introduction* (London: Sage Publications Ltd., 2007) 15–28, 44–47

Hellier, Jennifer. *The Brain the Nervous System and their Diseases – Vol. 1* (Santa Barbara: ABC-CLIO / Greenwood, 2014)

Hicks, Esther, Jerry. *Ask and it is Given* (Carlsbad: Hay House Inc., 2004) 114

Hill, Napoleon. *Think and Grow Rich* (Meriden: The Ralston Society, 1937) Chapter 13, part 1

Hillman, James. *The Souls Code: In Search of Character and Calling* (New York: Random House, 1996)

Koch, Liz. *The Psoas Book – 3rd Ed.* (Felton, Guinea Pig Publications, 2012)

Levine, Peter A. with Frederick, Ann. *Waking the Tiger. Healing Trauma* (Berkley: North Atlantic Books, 1997)

Carrying Water: Spirituality and Trauma. (https://youtu.be/8_pkgi-qdyQ, 2012)

McLeod, Saul. *Simply Psychology: Erik Erikson: Psychosocial Stages* (https://www.simplypsychology.org/Erik-Erikson.html, 2013)

Millon, T., & Davis, R.O. *Disorders of Personality DSM – IV and Beyond, 2nd Ed.* (Oxford: John Wiley & Sons, 1996 PsycINFO Database Record (c) 2016 APA)

Northrup, Christiane (https://www.drnorthrup.com/psoas-muscle-vital-muscle-body/2018)

Ornish, Dean. *Love and Survival* (New York: Harper Collins, 1999)

Scaer, Robert. *The Body Bears the Burden* (New York: Routledge, 2014)

Schenk, Paul. *Trauma Treatment (MPD/DID): A Few Definitions* (http://www.drpaulschenk.com/trauma_treatment.htm, 2017)

*Semper, Madeline. A Friendly Universe: Is the Universe a friendly place?...
by Albert Einstein.*
(http://afriendlyuniverse.blogspot.ca/2011/04/is-univers-
friendly-placeby-albert.html, 2012)

*Smith, Gary. Stand Up and Speak Out (New York: Sports Illustrated
Magazine, 12/17/2012) 72 - 84*

Timberline Knolls Residential Treatment Centre: *Trauma and PTSD
Recovery,*

Signs, Symptoms and Effects: What is Trauma? (http://www.timberline-
knolls.com/trauma/signs-effects/ 11/2017)

Van Der Kolk, Bessel. *The Brain keeps the Score: Brain, Mind, and Body
in the Healing of Trauma* (New York: Penguin Publishing Group, 2014)

Images by: Anne Babchuk and Paul Larosa.

CPSIA information can be obtained
at www.ICGtesting.com
Printed in the USA
LVHW090140180919
631411LV00002B/2/P